William Boyd Carpenter

The Great Charter of Christ

Being studies in the Sermon on the Mount

William Boyd Carpenter

The Great Charter of Christ
Being studies in the Sermon on the Mount

ISBN/EAN: 9783337086947

Printed in Europe, USA, Canada, Australia, Japan

Cover: Foto ©Lupo / pixelio.de

More available books at **www.hansebooks.com**

THE GREAT CHARTER OF CHRIST

BEING STUDIES IN THE SERMON ON
THE MOUNT

BY THE RIGHT REV.
W. BOYD CARPENTER D.D. D.C.L.
LORD BISHOP OF RIPON

NEW YORK
THOMAS WHITTAKER
2 & 3 BIBLE HOUSE
1896

thou canst not fathom. None can look on God's face and live. We know in part. Happiness is not in knowledge." Then there was silence while the young man's eyes recovered. And then said the Prophet, "Look once more, but look not on the heaven but on the earth." And the young man looked—and was glad ; for meadow, stream, and hill were bathed in happy sunlight. And the Prophet said, "What seest thou of heaven ? " And the youth answered, "I see the sunlight everywhere."

Then said the Prophet, "Be content. Mind not high things. Seek not to know mysteries. But seek goodness, purity, righteousness, and kindness, and thou shalt see God's sunlight everywhere ; and thou shalt find happiness within. Herein is the blessing of the Lord, that a man be satisfied in righteousness."

Then the youths left the Prophet : and, as they journeyed to their city again, he that had sought to know mysteries said : "I remember that it is written, 'In Thy light shall we see light.'" And the other, who had sought happiness in pleasure, made answer : " I, too, remember One who said, 'I am the Door. By me if any man enter in he shall be saved.'"

W. B. R.

CONTENTS

	PAGE
SOME ELEMENTARY PRINCIPLES OF THE RELIGIOUS LIFE	9
THE NEW HEAVEN FOR MEN	29
THE ARGUMENT OF THE SERMON	53
THE FIRST STEP TOWARDS HAPPINESS	75
EVERY SEVERAL GATE WAS OF ONE PEARL	99
KNOWN AND UNKNOWN INFLUENCE	131
THE INNER IS THE HIGHER	149
MARKETABLE RELIGION	185
THE PRAYER OF PRAYERS	205
WHAT IS PRECIOUS IN LIFE	231
PROSTITUTED ZEALOTISM	255
THE TESTS OF LIFE	277

SOME ELEMENTARY PRINCIPLES OF THE RELIGIOUS LIFE

1 Cor. xv. 46, 49

Howbeit that was not first which is spiritual, but that which is natural; and afterward that which is spiritual.

*　　*　　*　　*　　*

As we have borne the image of the earthy, we shall also bear the image of the heavenly.

SOME ELEMENTARY PRINCIPLES OF THE RELIGIOUS LIFE

ONE of the earliest forms of the religious consciousness is the sense of dependence. In the midst of the mighty and mysterious powers which surround him, man feels his weakness. He is the victim of inevitable pain, and of the nameless terrors born of ignorance. For the supply of his needs he is dependent on the bounty of that nature which can frown as well as smile. He seeks to grasp some hand of strength. He worships the power which is great and inscrutable, but his worship is largely the worship of weakness dependent on strength. This sense of dependence is an indispensable part of the religious consciousness, but unaccompanied by other elements, it may yield a very crude and distorted creed. If the God who is worshipped be only the God of power, the power may be exercised with caprice and favouritism. The history of religious beliefs shows us that under certain conditions men were prepared for the caprice of their gods, and were disposed to rely upon their favouritism. Even in the history of the Chosen People, this belief in favouritism had its place; and one of the tasks of the prophets was to dislodge it from the hearts of the people. When the people declared that the Lord was the God of Israel, they were not always giving utterance to faith in God as we understand it, but rather to a superstitious reliance upon the favouritism of Jehovah; and, therefore, the prophets denounced this as a blind confidence. Dependence is an essential part of the religious consciousness, but it may become the basis of a meagre and perverted creed. It needs a clear and steady teacher to inculcate a wholesome dependence without encouraging a weak, false, and selfish reliance. Superstitious confidence walks close behind the heels of faith.

1. What has the Sermon on the Mount to teach us about this dependence? Our Lord teaches dependence, and He teaches it most sweetly. "Behold the fowls of the air: for they sow not, neither do they reap, nor gather into barns; yet your heavenly Father feedeth them. Are ye not much better than they? Which of you by taking thought can add one cubit unto his stature? And why take ye thought for raiment? Consider the lilies of the

field, how they grow; they toil not, neither do they spin: and yet I say unto you, that even Solomon in all his glory was not arrayed like one of these. Wherefore, if God so clothe the grass of the field, which to-day is, and to-morrow is cast into the oven, shall He not much more clothe you, O ye of little faith? Therefore, take no thought, saying, What shall we eat? or, What shall we drink? or, Wherewithal shall we be clothed (for after all these things do the Gentiles seek): for your heavenly Father knoweth that ye have need of all these things" (Matt. vi. 26–32). As He speaks, Nature herself, with varied illustration, is giving emphasis to His utterances; for it is the spring-time. The flowers are in the land, and the time of the singing of birds is come. The beneficent hand which fills all things living with plenteousness is being opened. Earth is answering to the call of God. The promise of new life and fruitfulness is to be seen. The blossom is on the trees. Anxious solicitude may be banished. The power on which man depends is a power of beneficence. "Your heavenly Father knoweth that ye have need of all these things." Our dependence on God is natural and legitimate. Christ justifies such a dependence on our part by the holiest of sanctions. He treats it with a kind of inevitableness; for our reliance is the reliance of children on a father. His teaching is that it should need no effort to exercise a trust which ought to be a part of our very nature. It is a defect of our nature when we distrust. "If God so clothe the grass of the field, which to-day is, and to-morrow is cast into the oven, shall He not much more clothe you, O ye of little faith?" (Matt. vi. 30).

But in establishing the justification of our dependence on God, Christ protects us against the perversions of this confidence. He speaks so as to leave no room for superstition, or weak confidence, or hope of favouritism. He banishes the idea of favouritism in a clear and bold fashion by declaring the width and impartiality of the divine beneficence of that heavenly Father, who "maketh His sun to rise on the evil and on the good, and sendeth rain on the just and on the unjust" (Matt. v. 45).

He leaves no loophole for superstitious confidence; for He bases His teaching, not on any weak suggestion of an interference with the general order of nature, but on the sufficiency of that order, and on the all-sufficiency of the fatherly wisdom which is behind it; for reliance to be real must be reliance on God, and therefore on His wisdom, as knowing our needs better than we ourselves do. We thus get away from the mere barren idea of dependence. We depend on God, it is true, but our dependence is not limited to the power which gives food and raiment. It means reliance on the character of God. Our dependence is not on power alone, nor even on benevolence alone. It is on the wisdom and the love of Him who is our Father in heaven.

II. At this point we touch another great principle which is imbedded in the Sermon on the Mount. It is perfectly true that the hard facts of existence make us realise the importance of physical life. Food and raiment are needful; and the greater part of our time is spent in our efforts to secure them. But at the best these are only means of subsistence. The life which is sustained by bread is more than the bread which sustains it. Behind the things which are seen there are powers and forces which are greater than all outward forms. The outward world is beautiful; and Jesus Christ showed a spirit which rejoiced in its beauty. The Sermon on the Mount has in it that quality of joyousness in nature which has so often been wanting in religious teachers. There have been teachers who have felt it their duty to turn their back upon the radiance and laughter of the universe. The outward and visible world has seemed to them to be the foe of all that is spiritual. With Christ it was otherwise. The beauty of the world had its message to the soul of man. The facts and laws of the universe were instinct with meaning. The eye that would look into the face of nature might see more than mere beauty of form. The things which God had made, and the laws by which He wrought, could teach lessons. The fading leaf, the growing corn, the dying seed, the gorgeous flower, or the soaring bird, had voices which could reach the heart.

> " One impulse from a vernal wood
> May teach us more of man,
> Of moral evil and of good
> Than all the sages can."

The same reason which led narrow and limited teachers to eschew the contemplation of natural beauty, led Christ to include it in His vision. Men have shut their eyes upon flower and stream and star, because they hoped by this means that the eye of the soul would be opened to see more clearly the things of the spirit. Jesus Christ said: " Consider the lilies; behold the birds:" because He taught that the life was more than meat. The explanation is simple. Only let us remember the idea of ministry, and we shall see the significance of Christ's method. He asks us to see that the whole universe is pervaded by the spirit of ministry. The products of nature are for the needs of man. The fruits of the earth minister to life which is more than meat. But behind the sweet ministry of fruits and seasons there are the ceaseless love and care of Him who ordains this wondrous ministration, and who does so, understanding man's needs. So closely bound together are His love and the laws of beauty and ministration, that fully to understand anything would be to understand everything. All things are brought into the great wheel of ministration, and all things preach the love and wisdom which called them into being and activity. If man can only realise this, he will be saved from the pain of those myriad anxieties which torture his heart and mar his peace. But this deliverance from the torments of care and fear is not for peace's sake alone. God does not bestow faith on man that man may fall into a fat and sluggish indolence; but rather that, realising God's providence and God's character, he may realise that the life is more than meat, and that the order of ministration around him is designed that man may achieve the real purpose of his being. "Seek not," says Christ, "what ye shall eat or what ye shall drink." Seek not a life which is immersed in sordid cares and low ambitions. Seek that which is the life of all life. Seek that for which the ministry of providence is opening to you opportunities. Seek the kingdom of God and His righteousness. Transfer your ambitions (and as children of the heavenly Father you may safely do so) from the material to the spiritual. It is a matter of more moment that you should be righteous men and women than that you should be wealthy. To cultivate your moral nature is of more importance than to consider what you shall eat or what you shall drink. To be clothed with righteousness and meekness more befits the sons of God than to be clad in purple and fine linen. That with which God can clothe His children, the creatures of His hand, is more fair and seemly than all the splendour which the riches of Solomon can command. Higher than all outward and material pomp is the glory of the soul. Not what men have, but what men are, constitutes their real worth. Man is much better than the birds of the air, because he can grow in moral stature. The perfection of the flower is attained in beauty of colour and form. The perfection of the bird is its plumage and its song; but man can aspire to perfection of a higher order, even that of moral character. He may aspire to be perfect, as his Father in heaven is perfect.

In all this we discern the ethical quality of our Lord's teaching. He seems to say that character is everything. The basis of the calm trust of the child of God is to be found in the character of God. It is because of His fatherly character and wisdom that we may safely rest on His providence. Character is everything. The end of life, the purpose and aim of human existence, consists in the perfecting of character. It is the seeking of the kingdom of God and His righteousness. It is growing perfect as the Father is perfect. The relationship between man and God is not merely that of physical need and dependence. It is a relationship of the spirit and of the character. It finds its expression in moral resemblance. True fellowship is one of ethical affinity. The child must share the Father's spirit, and look upon life with his Father's eyes. If contentment comes when we can rely upon the wise providence and fatherly love of God, happiness is only found in the possession of moral disposition in harmony with God's character. This is Christ's proclamation to His disciples. Happiness is not found where the world seeks it, in worldly wealth, but in heavenly dispositions. Blessed—happy are the pure in heart, the meek, those who hunger for righteousness.

In realising this ethical relationship between God and man, we leave behind us the lower forms of the religious consciousness. In its crudest form, religion is the sense of dependence, the reliance of the weak upon the mighty Ruler or rulers or powers of nature for sustenance, protection and succour. This sense of dependence will always be present in religion.

Where there is no realisation of dependence, there can hardly be more than a pale shadow of religion. It was here that primitive Buddhism was weak; for it sought to create a religion from which a god who could or would help man was absent. But though this feeling of dependence is an almost necessary religious conception, the religion which does not go beyond it is crude and incomplete. In our childhood we may be content to recognise in our father the one whose hand provides our food; but even before we have left our childhood behind, we can realise that our moral growth is our father's care. Christ presses upon His hearers the need of realising this principle. Transfer your cares, He says, from the things temporal to the things spiritual. Seek not food, or raiment, or wealth, or gains. Dismiss the painful agitations and the vulgar cares of this sordid view of life. Turn your energies towards your moral cultivation. In doing so you will accumulate imperishable riches. All that your worldly care can bring will be the doubtful possession of riches of doubtful value. In the possession of the moral wealth of a noble and disciplined character, you possess that which can neither wither nor be stolen. What we have we must leave at the threshold of the grave. What we are goes with us into the other world. Riches will drop from our dying hand into the grasp of others. Character passes with us into the presence of God. Character is everything. This rather than worldly riches is the true end of life. The perfecting of this is the true purpose of God in life.

The moment this is realised, the whole conception of life changes. As long as we are blinded by worldly ideas, and falsely imagine that life consists in the abundance of the things which a man possesses, we are keenly alive to our own misfortunes. We are inclined to declare that life is not worth living, because we measure the worth of life by material standards. But when we begin to perceive that life is moral discipline, and its end the perfecting of character, we can be content with food and raiment, for we are sure that a nobler enrichment is going forward. The varied experiences of life are working towards that happiness which is above all earthly gain, because it is a happiness within ourselves, a happiness of disposition and character. If happiness consists in the fulfilment of the end of our being, human happiness must be found in growing into that likeness in which we were made, and in the attaining of which we reach our true maturity, and realise the purpose of God. It is thus that man is brought to understand what is meant by fellowship with God. Discord within and uneasiness of conscience mean want of harmony between what our lives are and what they ought to be: they reveal how far we are from fulfilling the true purpose of life: they show that we are out of harmony with the order of our life, that is with the will of God. Peace within means the end of this discord, the harmony of our will with God's will. When we desire what He desires for us, our moral dispositions are in sympathy with Him, and, this being so, we reach that stage of religious progress which may be called fellowship with God.

III. Here we touch another principle which works through the Sermon on the Mount. There have been those who have traced what they called Judaism or Legalism in this discourse. Many, who would not go so far as this, have yet a feeling that, though this sermon is very beautiful, the Gospel must be looked for elsewhere in the New Testament. These words of Christ are regarded by such as being a kind of incomplete statement of the Gospel of the kingdom. The sermon or discourse starts, in their view, midway between the teaching of the law and the declaration of the Gospel. In other words, it is thought that a flavour of legalism hangs round these words of our Lord. The theory which underlies these thoughts is, I believe, a false one. The nearer we can get to the words of Christ, the nearer we shall get to the truths of the Gospel. His teaching must be given the highest place in our hearts and our reverent regard. But has the idea that there is a tint of legalism in this discourse any foundation? It is difficult to understand how even superficial readers have ever supposed such a thing. Those who have endeavoured to grasp principles will know how completely the legalistic theory is undermined by Christ's teaching.

The legalist speaks of the obligation of the law, of man's duty to keep it, of the responsibility which our knowledge of the law entails, of the awfulness of the consequences which fall upon those who fail to fulfil it. The law and the penalities of the law are before his mind. Doom and judgment are the notes which he strikes. "This do, and thou shalt live," are the words which he sounds in our ears. This legalism has its place and its use. Rules are not the highest things to live by, but rules are useful till principles are understood. But "law maketh nothing perfect," as the apostle says. For if the perfection of man is the perfection of his character and moral dispositions, something more than the utterance of the law is needed to achieve it. The law may be holy, just, and good; but its holiness and goodness are powerless to make us love it or to transform our moral dispositions. The law can only indicate what is good. It cannot inspire the soul with a love of it. And yet moral perfection is unattainable if the heart cannot be touched with the love of what is good. What is the value of correct conduct, if the spirit within chafes against the law? It is not enough that we should observe the law. To reach inward moral perfectness we must love the law. To transform the schoolboy into the student, we must do more than supply him with books and insist on his mastering his task. We must fill him with a love of knowledge. Then the task is a task no more. The labour we delight in physics pain. The dutiful observance of the law is well as far as it goes; but it is far from the highest stage of the religious life. To reach that highest stage we must pursue holiness because we love it. We must seek goodness because we desire it. The love of what is holy, just, and true must have taken possession of our hearts. In other words, religion must be a power within us, and not a mere law without us. Now it is just this inwardness which our Lord teaches in the Sermon on the Mount. He claims that true religion must reach a higher level than that of external observance. With this the Scribes and Pharisees might be satisfied, but the Son of God could not rest content with anything so superficial. "Except your righteousness shall exceed the righteousness of the Scribes and Pharisees, ye shall in no case enter into the kingdom of heaven" (Matt. v. 20). He leaves us in no doubt as to the nature of that higher righteousness. The higher righteousness is the spiritual, inward righteousness. Ye have heard that it was said by them of old, "Thou shalt not kill; and whosoever shall kill shall be in danger of the judgment. But I say unto you, that whosoever is angry with his brother without a cause shall be in danger of the judgment." And as with the sixth commandment, so also with the seventh. The motions of the heart have their right and their wrong. If we are to test truly a man's nature, we must test it by the heart. The mere outside conduct may belie the heart. Many appear outwardly righteous, who have no inward love of righteousness. We can only know what a man truly is when we know his heart. The real man is the man within. He is found in the dispositions and desires which colour his character. Upon this our Lord insists with gravity and earnestness. True religion must find its home in the heart. What spirit has the man? This is the chief, the crucial question. If he is a truly religious man, a veritable subject of the kingdom of heaven, he must bring into his life the spirit in which the Father of all rules His kingdom. As the Father sends rain on the evil and the good, so the children of the kingdom must "love their enemies, bless them that curse, and do good to them that hate them" (Matt. v. 43, 44). Now this teaching is the very opposite of the teaching of legalism. This teaching carries us upward to that stage of religious life in which spiritual freedom is found. No man is a truly good man, according to Jesus Christ, who does not love goodness. Goodness followed under compulsion, or dread, or from a hard sense of duty which makes its pursuit a drudgery, is not the goodness of heaven. In the kingdom of heaven goodness is followed joyously because it is goodness. The doing of good is pure delight, because to do good is just nature to the children of the kingdom. This is spiritual liberty; this is the very opposite of that sense of bondage which is the accompaniment of legalism. In the possession of the spirit which loves all true, righteous and noble things, true happiness is found. There is no happiness in the spirit which is pining for worldly and sinful pleasures, while a cold and reluctant homage is yielded in the outward life to the conventional standards of righteousness. Happiness lies in heavenly dispositions. They are truly happy whose inner nature moves in harmony with the laws of the kingdom of heaven. It is with the declaration of this principle that Christ opens this discourse. "Blessed are the poor in spirit. Blessed are they that mourn. Blessed are the meek. Blessed are they that hunger and thirst after righteousness. Blessed are the merciful. Blessed are the pure in heart. Blessed are the peacemakers."

Such are some of the principles which lie imbedded in this Sermon on the Mount. Dependence as an essential element of religion is recognised; but it is redeemed from the danger of becoming an enervating superstition by the strong ethical spirit with which it is associated. But this strong ethical element, is saved from sinking into legalism, by the child-like spirit of the religion upon which our Master insists.

THE NEW HEAVEN FOR MEN

St. Matt. vi 32

Your heavenly Father.

THE NEW HEAVEN FOR MEN

IT was a saying of Edgar Quinet that a new heaven demands a new earth. The apostle, when he saw the vision of the renovation of all things, beheld "a new heaven and a new earth" (Rev. xxi. 1). "We, according to His promise," wrote another sacred writer, "look for new heavens and a new earth" (2 Pet. iii. 13). They come hand in hand. There is no new earth without a new heaven; and every new heaven brings a new earth. It is when the new sun is risen in the heavens that earth smiles in new beauty. The earth depends for its wealth and splendour upon the heavens. If the corn, wine, and oil cry to the earth for nourishment, the earth must cry to the heavens for the invigorating power. In human experience the same is true. Things are to us bright or dark, welcome or displeasing according to the eye with which we regard them. The glance of the eye is like the light of the sun in this, that it can invest what it looks upon with brightness. The same principle works in religious history. The law, if we may call it so, holds good in the religious consciousness of men. When men saw that heaven smiled, they carried the smile among their fellow-men. When in their judgment heaven frowned, fear bred distrust, and, as nothing is more cruel than fear, men looked on each other with cruel eyes. As was the heaven, so was the earth. As was their conception of God, so was their attitude to their fellow-men. The new heaven made the new earth. When they thought rightly and worthily of the Creator, they thought fitly and worthily of the creature of His hand.

Christ quickened men's hopes of a better age. The vision of an earth wherein should dwell righteousness was made clearer by His means (2 Pet. iii. 13). If sacred writers wrote of it, and devout people clung to the faith of it, it was through our Lord's influence and teaching that such enthusiastic confidence prevailed. But we cannot separate the new earth from the new heaven. Christ never divorced these two ideas. He never came preaching vague and baseless hopes of a golden age, and of a good time coming. He never spoke of earth apart from heaven, nor of man apart from God. He could assure men of the new earth, because He opened to them the kingdom of heaven. Foremost in His teaching, and made the source of every hope which might arise in the hearts of men, was His teaching about God. To understand the drift of His words and to catch the significance of His theory of the kingdom of God, we must first realise the conception of God which He puts before us.

This conception is comprised in a single word. He proclaimed God to be the Father of men. In the Sermon on the Mount, He used the word Father in this sense no fewer than sixteen times (Matt. v. 16, 45, 48; vi. 1, 4, 6, 8, 9, 14, 15, 18, 26, 32; vii. 11, 21). There is, moreover, no effort or straining after effect in the use of the word. It falls from His lips naturally and as a matter of course. God is the Father of all. The truth lies beyond all question. It is the primæval, nay, eternal truth. It has never been, it could never be otherwise. Any other theory is inconceivable. The whole universe would lose its brightness and its meaning, were the fact otherwise. It has been said that our Lord presented no theory of the universe. If this means that He offered no scientific account of its origin, and of its laws, it is true enough; but such a remark, if meant as a criticism and an objection, only means that Christ did not do what He neither pretended nor intended to do. But if it means that our Lord had no clear view, and offered to man no clear view of the meaning of the universe as it affects man's moral and spiritual nature and offered no clear conception of the spirit and order in which the universe was governed, then the objection has no basis in fact or truth. For nothing can be clearer or simpler than the view He presents of the relationship of God to the world and to man. In His reiterated declaration of the real, abiding, and necessary Fatherhood of God, He gives at once a picture of the sovereign order of the world and of the spirit and significance of the government of the universe as it affects man. In the simplicity and naturalness with which He declares this truth, we perceive that He adopts no self-conscious *pose*, attracting men's attention to Himself as the originator of this conception of God. He speaks of it as one who joins His hearers with Himself in the recognition of this conception as nothing novel or wonderful, but as a truth which every one does and must believe and acknowledge. He builds up no apology. He invents no syllogism. He never argues that it must be so. He takes for granted that in His own mind and in His hearers' minds it is so. Men are to let their light shine before men that they may glorify their Father which is in heaven (Matt. v. 16). They are to love and do good to their enemies that they may be the children of their Father which is in heaven (ver. 45). Ostentatiousness in benevolence brings no reward from the Father (Matt. vi. 1). Men may pray to the Father in secret (ver. 6). All men may unite in the prayer which addresses God as " Our Father."

It is needful to dwell on the frequency and naturally easy way with which our Lord introduces this conception of God that we may learn how real it was. It is not pretended that our Lord was the first who employed this word "the Father" to denote the Creator of the universe. The word had its place and its deep and true significance in the Old Testament. Isaiah had spoken of "the everlasting Father" (Isa. ix. 6). The later Isaiah had based one of his most pathetic and prayerful appeals to the Most High upon the fatherly relationship between God and His people. "Doubtless thou art our Father, though Abraham be ignorant of us and Israel acknowledge us not; thou, O Lord, art our father, our redeemer; thy name is from everlasting" (Isa. lxiii. 16). Jeremiah had declared God to be "a father to Israel" (Jer. xxxi. 9). Malachi had made this fatherly relationship the ground of a claim for homage and honour. "If I be a father, where is mine honour?" (Mal. i. 6). And, reaching a higher level still, he said: "Have we not all one Father? hath not one God created us?" (Mal. ii. 10). But passages like these, though they are full of significance and convey the hint of a truth capable of deep and expanding meaning, do not convey the truth with the same fulness and stability as do the words of our Lord. We feel that the words of the prophets may involve limitations and hesitations which find no place in Christ's utterances. Jeremiah, for instance, sees a fatherhood, but it is national, not universal. The fatherhood proclaimed by Isaiah is more that of a great Providence towards the world than that of individual tenderness. The later Isaiah (lxiii. 16) seems to emphasise, as Jeremiah does, the national aspect of the truth. And, in Malachi, it is the dignity of a Father, rather than His tenderness, which is the uppermost thought. We are reminded of the claims upon His children which the honourable title of Father carries with it. The thought of a Father's providing watchfulness and individual love is, to say the least, in the background. Thus, though the language of these prophets carries with it noble and just conceptions of God, they lack the fulness, richness, and tenderness of conception of Him which finds expression in the words of our Lord. They sing sweetly and well, but they give voice only to the prelude of that music which Jesus Christ gave with such strength and sweetness to the world. They give only the recitative. The air which went to the hearts of men was sung by Jesus Christ. In other words, we have approximations to the fatherly idea in the prophets. They shadow forth the thought in clear and strongly marked outline; but the thought lies in shadow still. It is to the true idea as the spectre on the Brocken is to the man whose shadow is seen among the clouds. It is human in form, but not in fact. The idea of the fatherhood of God does not take flesh and blood, if we may use the expression, till it is given to us by Christ (*cf.* John xiv.). When the fulness of the time had come, the fulness of the idea came with it; for only thus in its breadth, in its universal truthfulness, in its aptness to individual life and need was the thought of God as the Father in heaven given to Israel. Only then was this thought in its fulness given to Israel.

But had this idea of Fatherhood a place in the minds of men outside Israel? This opens a wide field of inquiry; but it may safely be said that the question cannot be settled by citing from Homer, Cicero, Seneca, and others, passages which speak of the Creator as Father and men as sons of the gods. Verbal resemblances are not always real likenesses. As we saw in the case of the prophets, the word Father may be used, but in a sense less full and less heart-satisfying than the sense in which it was used by Jesus Christ. Homer calls Zeus "the Father of men and gods." Men are described as bearing a resemblance to the gods. St. Paul, we all remember, quotes among the men of Athens the line which must have been familiar to many of them. "As certain also of your own poets have said, For we are also His [God's] offspring" (Acts xvii. 28). Man was the son of gods; and the gods were kindly, tolerant, magnanimous. "If you would be like to the gods," wrote Seneca, in language which bears resemblance to Christ's words, "bestow benefits even on the unthankful; for even upon the wicked does the sun arise, and to pirates all the oceans open" (*cf.* Matt. v. 45). But the spirit which breathes in the heart of such sayings is very unlike that with which our Lord inspired His words. Reliance, filial confidence, the flinging of the whole weight of the heart-life on the guidance and discipline of a loving Father-God, find no real place in such writers. Their faith, their ethical tone, falls very far below this, and below the level reached by Old Testament singers and prophets. Which of them ever touched the note struck by Jeremiah: "My Father, thou art the guide of my youth" (Jeremiah iii. 4)?

The Greek and the Roman are at their best far behind the Hebrew in their thoughts of God. But if Athens and Rome fall behind Judæa, it may be thought that Alexandria can present a loftier conception. Philo indeed, to take a writer who has been thought to have had contact with Christian ideas, gives us noble images of the Divine Being. "God," he says, "is the driver of the chariot, the pilot of the ship, the shepherd of the flock; over souls, and bodies, and thoughts, and words, and angels, and earth, and heaven, and things seen, and powers unseen, the Ruler of all things, the Father of the world." But beautiful as this is, it is by no means the uppermost thought of God in Philo's mind. The fatherly idea is subordinated (so far as it is a truly fatherly idea) to the thought of the greatness and incomprehensibleness of God: "The leading idea which, more than any other, seems to have taken possession of the mind of Philo and his contemporaries is, that the Divine Being is incomprehensible and invisible. There is nothing which he repeats so often as this, nothing for the sake of which he is so ready to pervert the meaning of Scripture." So wrote Professor Jowett, who tells us that Philo, led on by this theory, objected to the words, "I am the Lord thy God," as an incorrect expression. God was thus pushed away from men. He could not act directly on the world.

"Thrones, dominations, princedoms, virtues,

powers," as in some Asiatic court, surround the King of kings. "They are efficient causes in the hands of the world."*

Whatever there is of grace and beauty in these thoughts, they lack the divine touch which is felt in the teaching of Christ. Other teachers make us conscious of their theories. They are presented with obviousness and effort. We are in the atmosphere of argument. In Christ's teaching there is that inevitableness which is the stamp only of the highest. In His lips alone does the thought of the Father-God of all men become a deep, life-pervading, spiritual reality, fraught with ethical force.

But this conception of God must not be kept in the region of mere theory or theological speculation. Our Lord never treated it as such. It was a living truth, and it shed light upon all other truths. Life when seen in its light became a new thing. Life reflected back the smile of God as earth reflects the smile of heaven. Because the heaven which Christ disclosed to man was radiant with a Father's love, earth became new in the eyes of men; for earth was bathed in the same radiance. Dark, low, despairing thoughts of life became impossible. Life was worth living. The stern old Roman way

* "St. Paul's Epistles," by Professor Jowett, vol. i. pp. 395–399, new edition.

of quitting it was not possible, because the scorn of existence which found a place in philosophy was impossible to the man who realised that God was his Father. In other words, there was no tinge of pessimism in Christ's teaching because pessimism is impossible where the fatherly character of God is understood.

It is not that our Lord ignores the stern facts of life, or the darker and sterner facts of human sin. On the contrary, no guide of man has put his finger so unflinchingly upon human wrong-doing. None have searched so deeply into the hidden and poisoned sources of evil in man. He saw the evil not in action only, or in speech only. He saw it in the heart. He saw and He said that the evil could not be banished by gagging the tongue or covering the conduct. The tree itself must be made good if the fruit was to be good (Matt. vii. 16–20). He saw, and He frankly exposed, the hypocrisies of the conventionally religious. He saw the moral death which lurked behind the fairest shows of piety. He saw how good itself was made the minister of evil by the corruption of men. He saw the dead bones in the whited sepulchre. But, seeing all this, He did not despair of men, and He used no speech which might teach men to despair of life. When the facts of life and the evil in man are clearly seen, men are tempted to lapse into pessimism, unless at the same time the higher spiritual truths, the facts of heaven, are also seen. Insight into the nature of man, and vivid realisation of the ugly facts of existence, may plunge men into despair, or may lead men to those theories and practices in which hope itself seems to have grown hopeless. The consciousness of life without the consciousness of God ends in a pessimistic aversion to life. To eat of the tree of the knowledge of good and evil may end in despair.

"The Tree of Knowledge is not that of Life."

Those who seek to nourish themselves on knowledge without the knowledge of God eat but are not satisfied. They are not, and cannot be, fortified to look into the face of the world. To do so is to see the reasons of despair without perceiving the reasons of hope. To do so is to see the snakes uncoil around the face which looked so fair; and it is to be petrified by the sight, unless some kindly hand averts our gaze from the fatal fascination. Thus to avert the gaze has been the object of some philosophies and religions. Herein lies *one* difference between the teaching of Jesus Christ and of Gotama. The Indian teacher said, "Avert your gaze from life." Christ said, "Look life in the face." The one teaches us to avoid the world from despair, the other to overcome it by faith.

Some writers have found pleasure in dwelling on the parallels in circumstances and experience between our Lord and Gotama. The temptation, the forsaking of what was attractive, the parables spoken, and the first sermon preached, have been dwelt on. But while there are resemblances which none can deny, there is a difference of spirit and teaching which is evident to all who reflect. A comparison of the sermons will well illustrate what we mean.

Let us recall the Sermon of the Buddha, the preaching of which was regarded by his followers as the "inauguration of the kingdom of righteousness;" and as "a turning point in the history of their faith;" as "the day of Pentecost is regarded by Christians." The record of this sermon is given in the Dhammakakkappavattana-sutta or the foundation of the kingdom of righteousness. ("Sacred Books of the East," vol. xi. p. 139, &c.) It is briefly as follows— The Blessed One, *i.e.*, Gotama the Buddha, was once staying at Benares, at the hermitage called Migadāya. And there the Blessed One addressed the company of the five Bhikkhus and said: "There are two extremes, O Bhikkhus, which the man who has given up the world ought not to follow—the habitual practice, on the one hand, of those things whose attraction depends upon the passions, and especially of sensuality—a low and pagan way (of seeking satisfaction), unworthy, unprofitable, and fit only for the worldly-minded—and the habitual practice, on the other hand, of asceticism (or self-mortification), which is painful, unworthy, and unprofitable.

"There is a middle path, O Bhikkhus, avoiding these two extremes, discovered by the Tathagata, a path which opens the eyes, and bestows understanding, which leads to peace of mind, to the higher wisdom, to full enlightenment, to Nirvana!

"What is that middle path, O Bhikkhus, avoiding these two extremes, discovered by the Tathagata—that path which opens the eyes, and bestows understanding, which leads to peace of mind, to the higher wisdom, to full enlightenment, to Nirvana? Verily! it is this noble eight-fold path: that is to say:

> "Right views;
> Right aspirations;
> Right speech;
> Right conduct;
> Right livelihood;
> Right effort;
> Right mindfulness;
> Right contemplation.

"This, O Bhikkhus, is that middle path, avoiding

these two extremes, discovered by the Tathagata, that path which opens the eyes, and bestows understanding, which leads to peace of mind, to the higher wisdom, to full enlightenment, to Nirvana!

"Now this, O Bhikkhus, is the noble truth concerning suffering.

"Birth is attended with pain, decay is painful, disease is painful, death is painful. Union with the unpleasant is painful, painful is separation from the pleasant; and any craving that is unsatisfied, that too is painful. In brief, the five aggregates which spring from attachment (the conditions of individuality and their cause) are painful.

"This then, O Bhikkhus, is the noble truth concerning suffering.

"Now this, O Bhikkhus, is the noble truth concerning the origin of suffering.

"Verily, it is that thirst (or craving), causing the renewal of existence, accompanied by sensual delight, seeking satisfaction now here, now there; that is to say, the craving for the gratification of the passions, or the craving for (a future) life, or the craving for success (in this present life).

"This then, O Bhikkhus, is the noble truth concerning the origin of suffering.

"Now this, O Bhikkhus, is the noble truth concerning the destruction of suffering.

"Verily, it is the destruction, in which no passion remains, of this very thirst; the laying aside of, the getting rid of, the being free from, the harbouring no longer of this thirst.

"This then, O Bhikkhus, is the noble truth concerning the destruction of suffering.

"Now this, O Bhikkhus, is the noble truth concerning the way which leads to the destruction of sorrow! Verily! it is this noble eightfold path; that is to say:

"Right views;
Right aspirations;
Right speech;
Right conduct;
Right livelihood;
Right effort;
Right mindfulness; and
Right contemplation.

"This then, O Bhikkhus, is the noble truth concerning the destruction of sorrow."

Such was the teaching of the Buddha. It was a teaching which he declared was not handed down, but it arose within him. It gave him insight into that wisdom which is unsurpassed in heaven or earth. The light of it dawned, as the Buddha spoke, on the heart of one disciple, Kondañña by name, who then perceived that "whatsoever has an origin, in that is also inherent the necessity of coming to an end."

The teaching which we have here may be accepted as the authentic teaching of Gotama. "It would be difficult, we are told, to estimate too highly the historical value of this Sutta. There can be no reasonable doubt that the very ancient tradition accepted by all Buddhists as to the substance of the discourse is correct, and that we really have in it a summary of the words in which the great Indian thinker and reformer for the first time successfully promulgated his new ideas. And it presents to us in a few short and pithy sentences the very essence of that remarkable system which has had so profound an influence in the religious history of so large a portion of the human race." ("Sacred Books of the East," vol. xi. p. 140.)

It is not needful—indeed it is not right—to undervalue the character of this teaching. It proclaims the golden mean. It speaks, and speaks rightly, of the weak and mistaken methods of extremists. It realises that the mortification of the flesh is not the subjugation of the soul. It perceives the disastrous influence of uncontrolled desires. It grasps nearly, if not wholly, the truth that the kingdom of righteousness is within. Thus, as far as man's moral nature is concerned, its teaching is not far from the kingdom of God. But though this truth is so nearly grasped, and the unsatisfying character of the world is clearly comprehended, the whole effect of the teaching is disappointing. It has a pathetic rather than a heroic sound. The note of pessimism sounds through it all. The flower that blooms will die. The emotions of gladness, the tenderness of love, the invigoration of friendship, will pass into nothing. "Whatsoever has an origin, in it also is inherent the necessity of coming to an end." And as this is the case, the path of wisdom is to withdraw the affections and interests, the wishes and the hopes from all things, to live as those who are so detached from life that all desire and all hope of any abiding joy have passed away, and with them passes away also the capacity for suffering. It is quite true that there is much in the teaching of Buddha which the Western mind cannot adequately appreciate. The terms, the imagery, the modes of thought, are unfamiliar. It is not therefore on mere words that we should rely. The inferences from these may fail to do justice to the teaching of a teacher who was undoubtedly great, and whose character was worthy of admiration. But as we read the first sermon of Gotama without partiality and without prejudice, we receive an impression rather of sadness than of hope. We are brought into a place where it is darkness and not light. We are roused to no enterprise. We are not sent back to life invigorated or encouraged. Earth and life seem inexpressibly sad, and there is no opened heaven above our heads.

To turn from the sermon at Benares to the Sermon on the Mount, is to step from the sepulchre of the dead into the midst of the meadows, where the flowers are growing and over which the sun is shining. It is not that the moral standard is lower or the theory of life's duty is less severe. There is no flinching on the part of our Lord. He holds the flag of right high above us. He will have no morality which does not claim the whole heart and nature of man. But neither will He let man, weak as he is, forsake the field. While Buddha cries "Retire," Christ cries "Advance." While Buddha cries "Reduce the powers of affection and hope," Christ bids us live life fully, enlarging our capacities, strengthening while elevating our affections. The end which Buddha points to is the cessation of suffering. The end which Christ proposes to man is the perfection of character. The noble truths which Gotama proclaims are those concerning suffering, concerning the origin of suffering, concerning the destruction of suffering, and concerning the path which leads to this destruction. The noble truths which Christ declares are concerning the blessedness of the godlike character (Matt. v. 3–10), the power of influence and example (Matt. v. 13–16), the power of love (Matt. v. 43–48), the joy and the duty of trust (Matt. vi. 25–34), and the immovable stability of the true man (Matt. vii. 21–27). And all through these noble teachings the note of gladness and hope is sounded. Life is worth living. Happiness is not a delusion. It can be ours, and ours in such a form that no changes can rob us of its joy. The heart is full of a great and noble capacity of loving. If fixed on what is worthy, it can find unfailing and undecaying satisfaction. For over all there is the love of Him who is worthy to be loved. He ceaselessly watches over men. He supplies their need (Matt. vii. 7–10), He seeks their highest good (Matt. vii. 11), and He will certainly supply their earthly needs (Matt. vi. 30). It is this truth of the fatherly character of God which sheds the prevailing joyousness over Christ's sermon. It is the lack of this truth which leaves Gotama's sermon gloomy and sad. The difference is here. The sun shines in one; there is no sunlight in the other. The earth takes its colour from the state of the sky. The heaven is overcast as Gotama speaks. Christ's sermon reflects the light which He saw shining over all mankind.

THE NEW HEAVEN FOR MEN

That light was the light of a Father's presence. As M. Renan said, men wanted a Father, who should take count of their efforts. They wanted a Father, but they did not feel sure that God was their Father. They passed through stages of doubt and faith, as has been pointed out. "God is not a Father," they said. God is like a Father, they ventured to hope. "God is a Father," they at last learned to cry. This idea of the fatherhood of God, which is regarded by Professor Max Müller as specially characteristic of Christianity, was proclaimed at no time and in no place so clearly as it was taught by our Lord in His Sermon on the Mount. The Greek and the Roman missed its true significance. The Hebrew prophet hardly grasped the fulness of its meaning. The great Indian teachers knew nothing of it. But in the ears of the people who gathered in Galilee, Christ did more than proclaim it as a truth. He made it the main thread of His teaching. In doing so He made a new heaven over men's heads, and He made it certain that before long the new earth must appear.

THE ARGUMENT OF THE SERMON

St. John XVII. 24

Father, I will that they also whom Thou hast given me, be with me where I am; that they may behold my glory.

THE ARGUMENT OF THE SERMON

THE Sermon on the Mount has been called the Great Charter of Christ. Our interest in it lies in the moral and spiritual truths which it proclaims. These are independent of all questions of place or time. They are truths for every spot and for all time. It is therefore a matter of little moment to identify the exact place where the Sermon was delivered. Doubtless our imagination might form a more vivid picture of the scene and its surroundings if we were able to say with certainty of any place, "Here is the hill-side where the new law of the world, which is the eternal law of God, was given to mankind." But this pleasure of imagination is denied to us; for we cannot feel certain that the mountain of the Sermon has been identified. Probable conjectures and wild guesses have been made. The idea of what ought to be has, as usual, governed some minds in their determination of what was. Some reasoned that as on Sinai Moses gave the Law, so upon Sinai also should the New Covenant be proclaimed. Therefore, they concluded, Sinai was the mountain of the Sermon. This perverse mode of reasoning has provoked an equally perverse kind of criticism. It has been argued that the evangelists, with their Jewish prejudices, were ambitious that their Master should commence His mission with the same *éclat* and splendour with which the great legislator delivered his message to Israel; and therefore they invented a mountain from which, like Moses on Sinai, Christ gave His law. But reasonable people will not follow these methods. They will not be misled by any hypothesis of imaginative fitness. They will not read any sinister motive into the simple statement of a natural and consistent fact.

The narrative strains after no striking or suggestive effect in telling how Christ gathered His disciples round Him on the hill-side and opened His mouth and taught them there. The whole picture is simple and harmonious. Christ loved the mountain heights. He was wont to steal away to the quiet and solitude of the hills. There, removed from the noise and movement of life, isolated from the atmosphere of fret and passion in which men dwelt, on heights lifted above the lower levels He held communion with His Father. It was natural enough that He should draw His followers round Him on the heights He loved so well. It was consistent with His practice and His teaching that He should thus, as it were, shut the door for the moment, upon the din and turmoil of life, and in a quieter spot and under serener skies speak of the Father who saw in secret and would sustain their faith and courage in the public ways of life.

We may dismiss those guesses as to the locality of the mountain of the Sermon which are based on prepossession or prejudice. At the same time we may remember that there are many eminences in the neighbourhood of Capernaum which were suitable for the purpose. Robinson noted some dozen. A headland on the north of the town runs into the lake, and on one of the elevations of this hill our Lord may have gathered His disciples around Him when He opened His mouth and spoke to them of the things of the kingdom of God.

Around Him are gathered His disciples. It has been thought that He spoke only to a few. Some have sought to limit the company to the twelve. The indications of time are against this limitation. At this time the specific selection of the twelve had not formally taken place. The company assembled was the more numerous body of those who are described as disciples. Is the word to be taken in a very strict sense? Are we to suppose that our Lord spoke this Sermon only to those who had in some formal fashion avowed themselves as His disciples, and who might be regarded as belonging to a sort of initiated class? A further question must follow this. Was the teaching of our Lord designedly different from time to time according as He spoke to the initiated or uninitiated? It is quite true that our Lord varied His teaching. He spoke to men as they were able to bear it. As a wise teacher, He thought of the good of those to whom He spoke. There was no pædagogic love of display in His teaching. But, on the other hand, there was no reserve. There were not truths for the initiated, and other and different truths for the uninitiated. What He spoke to the disciples was truth also for all. His teaching of those immediately about Him became more distinct as they sought from Him explanations of what He had said. He does not alter or vary truth. He explains. He varies His mode of stating and teaching truth. The difficulty, if there be any difficulty here, is largely a created one. It is better to understand the word disciple in a broad and general sense, and take it to mean those who were attracted by His teaching and sought therefrom opportunities of hearing His instruction. The limitation of the company then is not an artificial or arbitrary one. It is rather what we may describe as a limitation of natural selection. Among those who gathered round Him were people who from their constancy in seeking Him might be called disciples. But even when He spoke to such, He often spoke in the hearing of more casual listeners. He spoke to His disciples, we read, in one case at any rate, in the audience of the people. He never spoke in the hearing of His disciples words which were not words also for the whole world.

It is necessary to dwell on this point, as there have been writers who have sought to rob from men some parts of Christ's teaching. By making overmuch of the distinction between the disciples and the multitude, they have introduced the notion of an esoteric and exoteric teaching on the part of our Lord; and from this the step has not been far to claim that portions of Christ's noblest and most universal teaching belong not to mankind, but to some few who hold a special *cachet* and upon whom has been bestowed the key of interpretation. It is for this reason that we need to remind ourselves that whatever may have been the character of those who heard the Sermon on the Mount, however true it may be that the Sermon evoked more intelligent response in some than it did in others, the truths which it declared were truths for the world. The teaching was not for the disciples alone. The Voice which told wherein happiness, duty, and the meaning of life consisted, spoke from the Galilean hill-side to the whole human race.

The Sermon itself has greatly exercised the minds of thoughtful and devout men. The first and most natural step is to compare the discourse in St. Luke (ch. vi. 20–49) with that given by St. Matthew (ch. v.–vii.). The differences strike us immediately. The Sermon given by St. Luke is much shorter. It diverges also from that of St. Matthew in several noticeable particulars. The Beatitudes are different in form. In St. Luke's discourse the sound of woe is heard side by side with the words of blessing (Luke vi. 24–26). Are we to conclude that the evangelists give us records of two distinct discourses, bearing that resemblance to one another which is not unnatural in the case of any teacher who does not hesitate to repeat world-needed truths? Or, did each evangelist give his own remembrance of some one or more of the discourses of our Lord? Were they anxious to give a faithful picture of the general teaching of Christ, rather than to be the reporters of some specific Sermon? Some critics have found what they believe to be various strata in the Sermon indicative of different epochs, and have concluded that the discourse, as we have it, is a compilation of recollections of more than one sermon. St. Matthew's version does not (so it is said) hang together. The evangelist has brought together in one elaborate Sermon utterances of our Lord made at comparatively widely separated periods. At the same time, it is said that the elaboration and order are too perfect to have been possible in one single discourse. These criticisms do not seem harmonious. But, like mutually contradictory pleadings in a court of law, they have their separate force. There is no objection to our supposing that the evangelist grouped his remembrances into the forms which were natural and easy to himself. It has long ago been noticed that Matthew edited, if we may be allowed the expression, the discourses of our Lord. The question whether the whole Sermon contained in the three chapters of St. Matthew (ch. v., vi., vii.) was delivered as it now stands or was compiled from separate sermons, is of less importance than the question whether we have in these chapters the genuine teaching of our Lord. And on this question there is practically little doubt. "It is admitted," says Keim, "on all sides, even by Bauer and Strauss, that this address undoubtedly contains a great number of genuine, vigorous, and striking utterances of Jesus, a veritable microcosm of the new higher conception of the universe" (Keim, vol. iii. p. 17,

T. T. F. L.). "It contains," he adds, "a treasure of such original and pregnant sayings of Jesus as He actually delivered in the springtime of His teaching." It is possible that some portions of the Sermon may have belonged to a later time, but even on this point there is some doubt. For instance, it is possible that one portion of the Sermon was spoken to the people generally, and that afterwards our Lord spoke more fully, though on the same lines, to the more intimate circle of His disciples. But, even after making all allowances, we may be satisfied that we have in these chapters of St. Matthew's Gospel the substance of the genuine teaching of our Lord. The hand of the evangelist may have edited or compiled the Sermon from his recollections; the words, and what is more, the spirit of Jesus Christ are here. The discourse, as recorded by St. Matthew, may have been given in different portions at different times, but read as a whole the chapters display order and connection. The Sermon passes from point to point, and each new section rises naturally out of its predecessor, while all so succeed one another as to lead with persuasiveness and inevitableness to a vigorous and striking conclusion.

The Sermon has in it an ethical order, akin to that dramatic harmony, which characterises the highest kinds of spoken addresses.

THE ARGUMENT OF THE SERMON

We must follow out this order, or we shall lose the full force of our Lord's teaching. Much good may spring from the study of special portions, or even of isolated verses, for these are instinct with living meaning. But the highest gain belongs to those who seek to grasp the general drift of the whole, and who thus gain an insight into the spirit of our Lord's words; for whether the Sermon as we have it was a single discourse or a compilation from several, it is given to us by St. Matthew as a compacted whole which represents the early teaching of Christ.

It was thus, then, that our Lord taught His disciples.

The seat of true happiness lies within man, for happiness does not consist in the things which are the mere accidents of life, but in those things which belong to its essence, that is, in the moral dispositions and in the spiritual attitude of man (Matt. v. 1–12). But everything which has vitality in it is also diffusive, influential, reproductive. The inner ethical dispositions must reveal themselves for the benefit of the world (ch. v. 13–16). But though the inward is the true kingdom of man, there is no real hostility between this conception and loyalty to the law. On the contrary, the realisation that the abode of happiness and the throne of man's kingdom are within, deepens and intensifies the significance of the law and the prophets. The least thing becomes great in the light of a universal law (ch. v. 17-19). The conception of righteousness is elevated wherever the spiritual conception of life is realised (ch. v. 20). Though no act of wrong can be specified, murderous, licentious, reckless, and vindicative dispositions are standing violations of the law (ch. v. 21-42). Nay, mere negative virtue is no virtue at all. Not to do evil is not the whole law. To limit the obligations of law by artificial or geographical boundaries reveals a disposition which has missed the spirit of the law. There is a law behind the words of law, and that is the law which the spirit of the law imposes upon the spirits of men. Not to do harm would be a poor result for any divinely given law to achieve. The true son of the law will catch the spirit of the lawgiver. He will not be satisfied to love his neighbour and hate his enemy. He will catch the spirit of Him whose love falls in bounty upon all. He will seek to be perfect as His Father is perfect (ch. v. 43-48). Such is the higher life which a deep and spiritual interpretation of life and law enforces.

But this higher life is above all earthliness of conception, and excludes worldliness of motive. It is hostile to the spirit of ostentatious piety. It has its roots within and above. Its life is not derived from the love of applause. The disciple must, therefore, beware of any ambitious display of a piety higher than that of others. He must distinguish between the real and unreal. The real arises from genuine love of the heavenly Father, the unreal from love of the applause of men. But alms, prayer, fasting, which are well enough in themselves, may spring from unworthy motives, and so prove, religiously speaking, unreal (ch. vi. 1–18). The line which divides the real from the unreal is a line which is drawn in the heart of man. As happiness lies in the disposition, goodness and badness are to be found there also. The worldly, fame-loving, lucre-loving disposition leads to unreal piety (ch. vi. 16). All the life is coloured by the spirit or disposition of the man (ch. vi. 17–23). It is vain to attempt to reconcile the irreconcilable. If a man's heart goes out to the world, his piety will only be awkward, unnatural, unreal, a burden bound upon him, not a necessity of his life and nature (ch. vi. 24). Nay, consider how far this worldly spirit is from the truly religious spirit. That spirit is filial. Life is apportioned by a wise Father, who knows and understands. To live in the spirit of goading anxiety is to distrust the Father's care; to live for the accidental rewards and applause of life is to insult and forget it. Nay, all the fume and fret of life is vain; it can achieve nothing. It needlessly disturbs the soul, which should leave to God the Father the ordering of its life. The disciple's mind should be set upon moral and spiritual advance; it would then have no time or scope for lesser and lower things (ch. vi. 25–34). The higher life dismisses the snares of worldliness, whether they come as ambitions or anxieties. It has one aim—righteousness, because it has One whom it seeks to resemble, the Father in heaven (ch. vi. 33 and v. 48). But even the earnest pursuit of righteousness is not without its snares for weak and self-ridden men. The disciple may escape the temptation to display his piety to win the applause of men, but he may allow his ideas of righteousness to lead him into censorious and uncharitable moods. He may judge others harshly and unlovingly (ch. vii. 1–5). He may, in his very zeal for righteousness, sin against the law of love. He may seek good by means which are not good. He may make his piety the slave of uncharitable thoughts and unruly passions. He may make the precious jewel of his own religious life the prey of prejudices and unbrotherly judgments (ch. vii. 6). Thus there are snares round the path of piety. Egotism may enter into it, either in the guise of ambition or in that of unbrotherly arrogance. It needs the help of a Father's hand to guard against these snares. But here again the principle of the inwardness of life will help. Happiness is within, the throne of righteousness is within, the Holy of Holies may be within; for inward strength is given to those who ask and seek (ch. vii. 7-10), by Him who, if He gives rain to the evil and the good, will not withhold His Spirit from those who hunger and thirst after righteousness (ch. vii. 11). The disciple, in proportion as he understands the Spirit of God, will cultivate the habit, not of judging men, but of trying to understand them by putting himself in their place (ch. vii. 12).

Thus, though the kingdom of happiness and heaven is within, there are inward temptations also, which arise out of untrained, worldly, selfish, and arrogant affections. It is not easy to do right. It is hard indeed to do right in the right way. We may do good from worldly motives, so close beside one another are piety and worldliness. But even if we escape these, there remains the last and subtle temptation of eager and earnest souls—the temptation to promote good in ways which are not good, to cast pearls before swine, to do evil that good may come (chs. vi. and vii. 1-6). He who would be a disciple indeed, therefore, will find that he must not only abandon worldly things, he must abandon self, so strait is the gate and narrow the way of true life. Many miss it because they are content with piety on the outside, with piety of words, with plausible reasonings for evading the spirit of the law of God (ch. vii. 13, 14). But all who, even under the pretext of righteousness, set aside the clear rule of righteousness and love, who would either do wrong or do right wrongly, who would not do wrong and yet would wrongly win, are false prophets. No matter how urgently they plead the righteous cause as an excuse for unrighteous deeds, they are bad weeds and injurious growths in the garden of the Lord (ch. vii. 15–19). The test of men is their conduct, their deeds; no amount of religious talk, no pious intentions can alter the truth that the tree is known by its fruit, and a man's disposition by his conduct (ch. vii. 20–23). The time for testing men will come; then, not those who have used religious language, or who have done certain religious actions, or who have promoted with zeal and eagerness religious objects, will stand the test. Only those who have been truly and really religious, who have translated the law into their lives, who have practically carried out their religious principles, inwardly by loving them and outwardly by living them, will abide unshaken in the hour when the house is assailed by flood and tempest. Then the difference between the real and the unreal will be made manifest. Then the religion which is theory, opinion, sentiment, will be found wanting, while the religion which is practical in heart and thought and life will remain unmoved (ch. vii. 24–27).

The teaching thus given is clear and explicit. We are carried naturally from point to point. However it has come to pass, the order and connection are sustained. Instruction, exposition, and caution are used in teaching concerning man's happiness, character, and destiny. The discourse is by turns calm and lucid, animated, earnest even to irony. It is simple and profound when it sets forth principles: it becomes more vivid and oratorical as it deals with their practical application. It is less didactic and less antithetical as it moves towards the close. The points have been made clear: the argument is complete: the fire kindles: the passion of persuasion is felt: the climax is reached in the graphic setting forth of the fates of moral reality and moral unreality (ch. vii. 24–27). All this is natural. It follows the lines in which a noble address inevitably develops. The differences in tone and treatment between the earlier and later portions of the Sermon have been taken to indicate that we have an earlier and a later Sermon; but may not these differences be variations natural to the development of the address? The latter part differs from the earlier, we are told. "Instead of thesis and antithesis, there is simply a vigorous antagonism, overthrowing and then building up; instead of doctrine, practice; instead of attack upon doctrine, the rejection of practice; instead of incisive, quietly acute, and comprehensive brevity, we have wealth of detail on a limited canvas, an artificial ostentation of refrain, a more agitated and excited mood, and an inexhaustible play of annihilating irony."* We should prefer to omit from this description some exaggerated epithets, and to speak of a bolder use of refrain, a more earnest mood which expresses itself now in irony and now in vehemence. But having done this, we may readily accept the description as expressing with fair exactness the difference between the early and the later parts of the Sermon. But are not these changes characteristic of the growing warmth and persuasiveness of the discourse? Does not the speaker, after calm, careful, incisive analysis and exposition, pass on to the work of application and persuasion? Have we not here qualities which indicate one great, harmonious, varied, but purposeful discourse? The truths are not less true, even if this is not the

* Keim.

case; but the oratorical completeness displayed—if I may use the expression—ought to count for something in our judgment on the matter. The Sermon has too often been regarded as a series of isolated and mutually irrelevant utterances. It has been treated as a treasury of choice sayings, while in fact it is a connected address, in which teaching, argument, and impassioned appeal are used with rich variety, but with skilful restraint, while the one aim and purpose has never for an instant been lost sight of. It is a Sermon on human character in relation to God and life. To be possessed of a truly noble character is to have happiness, and to make this character felt in the world is to promote the moral health and happiness of mankind (ch. v. 1-17). But a truly noble character must have nobility in its very roots, and in its unseen, inward processes: its throne as well as its sceptre must be pure (ch. v. 18-32). It must be self-restrained, calm, patient, affectionate, and compassionate (ch. v. 33-47). In one word, it must be godlike (ch. v. 48). It must be above the littleness of vulgar ostentation; it must be simple, natural, and trustful in its piety (ch. vi. 1-18). It must be single-minded (ch. vi. 19-24). It must realise the bounty and wisdom, the glorious and magnanimous love which surrounds life (ch. vi. 25-34). It must be tolerant and charitable, hard to self and large-hearted to the world, making allowances for others (ch. vii. 1–6). It must be ready for the conflict, reliant on God (ch. vii. 7–12), not afraid of difficulty and hardship, strenuously honest, wholly real. Its stability will be proved in trial. In the experience of life many characters degenerate, lose their force, and have their integrity undermined. The noble character proves itself in endurance. It is unterrified and unseduced. When others give way before the storm or the snares of the world, it holds fast its integrity. It stands like a tower, four-square to all the winds that blow. It is founded on a rock (ch. vii. 24–27). It is a strong, noble, human character—most noble in that it is patient, unselfish, gentle and loving. It is strong, because, being aware of its weakness, it is made divinely strong by divine help (ch. vi. 9–14; ch. vii. 7–12). It is stable, for though it is human, it humbly and trustfully reckons that God is its Father. It has a filial spirit, for it realises that a son is dependent on the Father. It has a filial spirit also in this, that it strives to realise the Father's character in itself, and reckons that it is its noblest privilege and joy to live this life as a son of God.

We easily perceive the spirit of a great moral charter in teaching like this. After a fashion—lofty, complete, unique—Christ proclaimed that God was the Father of all. He was not merely like a Father: He was a true Father of man and of men, of the individual and of the race. His fatherhood was not merely the fatherhood of power and of dignity. It was the fatherhood of real relationship, of care, guidance, discipline, education, of tireless love, and of a changeless loving purpose. It went beyond a fatherhood of mere providence. It involved more than the care which gave the sunshine and the rain. It was a fatherhood which meant a real, definite, moral purpose towards men. That purpose was their education: it was the discipline and training which corrected their weaknesses, evoked their trust, and stimulated their ambition. It set before them a goal loftier and more spiritual than men had dreamed of. That goal was, to grow like to Him who was their Father. The goal was character. In that lay the true stability and happiness of life. Only when man could wake in God's likeness, could completeness and satisfaction of life be realised (Ps. xvii. 15).

THE FIRST STEP TOWARDS HAPPINESS

St. Matt. v. 3

Blessed are the poor in spirit.

THE FIRST STEP TOWARDS HAPPINESS

BLESSED are the poor in spirit; for theirs is the kingdom of heaven. Such is, according to St. Matthew, the first beatitude. St. Luke gives his blessing in a less qualified form. Blessed be ye poor (Luke vi. 20). In this, it has been said, we have a frank and bold commendation of poverty as such. The poor man is happier than the rich man. The very lack of the good things of life constitutes happiness. Such in the view of some is the meaning of the beatitude as given by St. Luke. Antagonists of Christianity have maintained this meaning, because they found in it as they imagined a weapon against the faith. They wished to show that Christianity had no true sympathy with the struggling classes; and they pointed to this beatitude and said, "See how Christianity seeks to keep you in an ignominious contentment by telling you that you are happier without wealth and comfort. Religion seeks to make you tame and acquiescent in your miseries by promising you great things in an unknown and future state. It plays into the hands of the prosperous, who wish you to forego enjoyment here and now, in the hope of shadowy joys in a shadowy kingdom. In order to keep you from disturbing the possessions which they enjoy in this world, they promise you possessions in a realm they little believe in, seeing that they do not willingly encounter the poverty which, in their theory, is necessary to win it."

1. There is no reason in support of this view. But before we condemn it as a forced and false gloss upon the words of Christ, we may well ask whether there is not some excuse for it. The dominion of Christianity in the world for many centuries has been great and wide. The hopes of a golden age which the supremacy of Christianity would bring have been doomed to disappointment. The struggling classes have not found themselves transported to a realm of cloudless skies. In sorrow and disappointment they have seen that Christianity was the creed of the ruling classes. They have seen more; they have often seen that in the mechanism of society, religion was regarded as a power on the side of privilege. They heard a gospel which declared that there was a sort of divine appointment in things as they were. They

heard sermons on texts, which seemed to mean that all effort after improvement was profane. They began to identify the creed of Christendom with the customs of society. They accepted the interpretation of religion which the well-to-do classes practically adopted. They took their view of Christianity from the lives and habits of those who professed and called themselves Christians. Can we wonder at it? Can we wonder that a misinterpretation, sanctioned by the habit of Christendom, should be accepted as the real meaning of Christ's words by those who felt that fashionable creed and fashionable custom alike were against them? We have here only another instance of what Christianity has suffered at the hands of Christians.

But no excuse or explanation of a false interpretation can justify our accepting it. Even supposing that the words of our Lord were, as St. Luke gives them, well-nigh unqualified words, and that He indeed said, " Blessed are the poor," there is no ground for declaring Him to have been void of sympathy with poverty or to have used the words to soothe the unfortunate and indigent into convenient contentment. It cannot escape the reader of St. Luke's version of the Sermon on the Mount that there are woes joined with the blessings, and that the same voice which says, "Blessed are the poor," says also, "Woe unto you that are rich; for ye have received your consolation." Surely it is unreasonable to construe such utterances as these into a kind of protective apology for the wealthy classes. The words sound more like the vehement language of the indignant St. James, who saw the oppression of the poor, the indifference and the dishonest heedlessness of the rich, and wrote, "Go to now, ye rich men, weep and howl for your miseries that shall come upon you" (James v. 1).

II. Are we then to interpret the words as an attack upon the rich? Are we to believe that our Lord declared simply and in unqualified fashion the superiority of poverty as such over riches as such? Views of this kind have been held by many teachers at different epochs of history. For example, in the time of our Lord, the Ebionite taught the advantages of poverty. Did our Lord adopt this Ebionite conception?

Those who have caught the spirit of Christ's teaching will hardly believe this. In our Lord's view, outward circumstances were as nothing compared with inward dispositions. The Son of the heavenly Father accepted the Father's will and providence. Whatever was His lot, whatever hard or happy experiences were His, there was something to be gained from all. Inward strength increased in the use of all life's experiences. But for this purpose, the soul must carry itself in equal indifference towards the wealth and poverty of life. The realisation of the kingdom within made the external conditions of life entirely subordinate. They were matters in which choice had no place. The only choice of the soul was the doing the Father's will. The conditions under which that will was to be done were left in the Father's hands.

The self-chosen poverty of the Ebionite was inconsistent with this teaching; for, in the Ebionite view, poverty itself brought sanctification. In our Lord's view outward circumstances were powerless of themselves to produce inward holiness. When the inward disposition was that of the child, outward circumstances, whether they brought straitness or affluence, would be made means of increased strength of soul. In the language of St. Paul, "All things work together for good to them that love God" (Rom. viii. 28).

We may take it then that our Lord taught that there was no magical virtue either in poverty or riches. As in the hands of Apollo all instruments were alike, so in the heavenly Father's hands all circumstances of life would make music in the soul.

Both riches and poverty brought temptation, but the power to encounter temptation came from God. Victory over temptation is not found in change of circumstance, but in spirituality of heart.

The followers of Christ did part with their possessions. Rich men abandoned their wealth for the kingdom of heaven's sake; but among those who have done so, they only did it rightly who forsook their wealth because of the greater love which possessed their heart. The spiritual disposition was there. The love of Christ constrained them. They thought not of their merit or of their gain. They had no weak views of the abstract superiority of indigence. They had no belief in the magic of altered circumstances. They were not materialists enough to believe that aversion to spiritual things could be transformed into love by a change of material conditions. They were moved by a larger love, which esteemed earthly gain but loss for the excellency of the things of God. Their renunciation of riches was the consequence, it could not be the cause, of their faith and love.

III. But the difference between St. Matthew and St. Luke remains. How are we to explain it? St. Luke says simply, "Blessed be ye poor." St. Matthew says, "Blessed are the poor in spirit." Are we to see in St. Luke's version the influence of

Ebionite feeling? In other words, are we to suppose that though our Lord did not adopt the Ebionite position, St. Luke, being himself tainted with their views, gave an Ebionite turn to this beatitude? To give consistency and force to this view, it would be necessary to show that a distinct Ebionite tone was manifested, not in a doubtfully interpreted sentence here and there, but throughout the whole of St. Luke's Gospel. That is, it would be needful to show that, according to St. Luke, our Lord taught, not the indifference of wealth or poverty, but the positive evil of one, and the positive good of the other. In short, it would be necessary to prove that on this point there was a deep and radical difference of principle between St. Matthew and St. Luke. It may be true that each evangelist writes his story from his own view-point. His own personal character and special interest combined to give shape to his manner of telling his story. But even this aspect of the matter may be given an exaggerated importance, and fancy may attribute to its influence more than in the circumstances of the case was likely. Yet even when we allow much for the influence of individual character, it seems unlikely that the evangelist would venture on a strong and decided perversion of the very principles laid down by our Lord. This is a question which the ordinary reader is almost as competent to decide as the learned critic, for it is a question, not of the exact and erudite interpretation of difficult passages, but of the general tone and tenor of the Gospel of St. Luke. In St. Luke we meet with teaching which speaks of the snares of wealth, and the dangerous tyranny which riches may get over the heart of man. Our Lord is represented as saying, "How hardly shall they that have riches enter into the kingdom of God" (ch. xviii. 24). He speaks the parables of the Rich Fool (ch. xii. 16-21) and of Dives and Lazarus (ch. xvi. 19-31). But the warnings against the deceitfulness of riches are equally clear in St. Matthew (ch. vi. 19; xiii. 22; xvi. 24-26; xix. 23); and the passages in St. Luke are, like those in St. Matthew, directed against the love of riches, rather than against the possessors of riches; against those who have allowed themselves to be vulgarised, morally degraded, and heart-hardened by wealth, and not against the wickedness of riches as riches. The teaching in fact is spiritual, not material, in both Gospels. The evil of the world is not in the possession of more or less of its material produce or advantages; the evil lies in the soul which suffers these things to carry it away captive, which becomes the slave, instead of being the master of earthly things. The tenor of both Gospels seems to me to be the same on this subject. There is none of that popular confusion of thought between the man and his circumstances. There is no suggestion of the theory that because a man is poor he must be good, and because a man is rich he must be bad; or, *vice versa*, because he is rich he must be good, and because he is poor he is sure to be bad, which is so popular among thoughtless or unspiritual minds. A rich man needs much grace. That is true; and so our Lord teaches that the things which are impossible with men are possible with God (St. Matt. xix. 26 and St. Luke xviii. 27). The power of the divine love would be able to show itself in giving victory over self to rich and to poor, teaching the rich man not to trust in uncertain riches (1 Tim. vi. 17), enabling the brother of low degree to rejoice in that he is exalted, and the rich in that he is made low (James i. 9, 10).

It is with the remembrance of this general tenor of teaching which pervades St. Luke's Gospel that we must approach the beatitude. "Blessed be ye poor." He does not say, "Blessed are the poor," as though mere poverty were a blessing, for poverty, like wealth, brings sore temptations and much painfulness of which wealth knows nothing. Poverty may become a means of blessing, no doubt; but this is very different from saying that it is a good in itself. It is only a good, and a means of good, to those who have reached that condition of soul in which the supremacy of spiritual things is so great that worldly conditions are of comparatively little moment. Only those who view earth from the threshold of heaven are able to derive from either riches or poverty their powers of spiritual helpfulness. Therefore, our Lord does not say, "Blessed are the poor." But rather, speaking to His disciples whose dispositions He knew, He spoke these words, for we read, "He lifted up His eyes on His disciples and said, Blessed be ye poor; for yours is the kingdom of heaven." It is not every poor man who is blessed in his poverty, though all everywhere may find in their circumstances a blessing. It is the poor man who has risen above his poverty, who knows that a man's life does not consist in the abundance of the things that he possesses, who realises that the life is more than meat, it is such a poor man who can find the blessing in poverty. The disciples, most of them poor in circumstances, were yet blessed, because they were already those who were, to use St Matthew's language—poor in spirit.

IV. Blessed are the poor in spirit; for theirs is the kingdom of heaven. But who are the poor in spirit? What is meant by this being poor in spirit? Does Jesus Christ counsel His disciples to be feeble, shrinking, timid beings? Is poor in spirit the same as poor-spirited? It ought to be needless to answer this question; but unfortunately there are people in the world who have a genius for misinterpretation, and there are many besides whose minds are of a slatternly order, and who snatch up words without any effort at discrimination. Such people can misunderstand anything, because there is very little which they do understand.

There is no approval of poor-spirited characters here. The simplest way to grasp its meaning is perhaps to consider its opposite—*i.e.*, the moral distortion of being lifted up in spirit. This uplifted spirit is the spirit of self-exaltation which filled the heart of Nebuchadnezzar when he contemplated the glories of the great Babylon which he had built. This is the self-satisfied spirit of those whose hearts are as fat as brawn, who call their lands after their own names, and look at everything through the medium of their own self-importance. For such the world has no significance except as it affects their interest or their convenience. This is the radical spirit of worldliness; for it is the spirit which makes self the centre of everything. This spirit is the seed ground of sin. All kinds of wrong become possible to the man who makes his own pleasure or aggrandisement the supreme rule of his life. Conscience has little place in the heart of the man who makes self the axis of reference in all his conduct. This inflated egotism is flat against the order of the universe, and essentially hostile to the kingdom of God. It is in one sense the starting-place of evil; it is in another sense its climax. Egotism in moral life is the cause of most of the heedlessness and sinfulness of the world; and yet, it is only after a prolonged indulgence of selfishness that the humane and kindly instincts of nature are destroyed. The evil principle of self works till all the finer, better, and purer feelings and aspirations are brought to naught. It stands out then as the naked antagonist of all that is good.

The divine kingdom is covered by the very opposite principle. "I, yet not I" is its motto. We exist not for ourselves. There is no overmastering egotism, no proud isolation, no self-exaltation or self-seeking in the spiritual kingdom. The poor in spirit have nothing of their own; they are emptied of self; they are dead to self.

"None of us liveth to himself" is the language of all things which follow the order of God. This being so, they only find themselves in others. They find their life in losing it. They find love in giving it. They find themselves in not thinking of themselves. He who does not think of self is poor in spirit. The poor man is the man who has nothing of his own.

THE FIRST STEP TOWARDS HAPPINESS

The poor in spirit is the man who has nothing of his own, no self-seeking in his motives and fancies. This spirit is well exemplified in John the Baptist. When men came asking him, "Who art thou?" he acknowledged nothing about himself; he had no description to give of himself; he claimed no name among men; he did not call himself, "Elias," or "that prophet;" he sought to be the voice of God, and that voice only (John i. 19–23). He, who was ready to decrease that the true messenger of God might increase, was content to be nothing in the world, if he might only pass on God's message to men.

We can understand the happiness of this attitude. The man is absorbed in the work—the God-given work—before him. He has no leisure to pause and ask what the world thinks of him. There is a real work to do, and he is alive to its importance and to the necessity of turning his whole energy into it. The work has to be done; the trust must be discharged; the criticisms of the world, whether favourable or unfavourable, are of little moment. Egotism has so small a place in his spirit that he is neither uplifted nor depressed by the words of men's lips. His soul is set on other things. He seeks the kingdom of God, and no kingdom of self—and it is in the emancipation of self from self that he finds that divine kingdom. He loses himself to find himself.

He is nothing in his own sight, but for this reason the kingdom of God is his. He who grasps for self ends by grasping nothing but self; he who grasps only at right, grasping nothing for self, finds the kingdom of God within his grasp. He who lives as having nothing is the one who possesses all things. It is to the poor in spirit that the blessing of the truest possession comes. Theirs is the kingdom of God, says Jesus Christ. "All things are yours," writes St. Paul. The two thoughts run parallel. The possession of all things belongs only to him who understands what true possession means. "It is mine" in the language of the world means this thing belongs to me and to none else. "It is mine" in the language of truth means "I draw from this thing the good which it is capable of imparting." The book is the property of the man who buys it. It is the possession of the man who masters it. The force, the power, the knowledge, the virtue of things cannot be said to belong to him who has rights over them which he has never exercised. They belong to him who derives benefit from them. They belong to him into whose nature they have transmitted their life-power. They belong not so much to him who owns them, as to him who has made them his own. Now the first condition of achieving this is the getting rid of all egotism and self-caused prejudice. "To unlearn what was naught" was, according to the old philosopher, one great part of his life-work. The approach to work or study must be with a free mind. Preoccupation, like prejudice, is a hindrance to knowledge. The ceasing from self is as needful in the pursuit of knowledge as it is in the order of religion. The mind filled with prejudice, vitiated by preconceptions of which it is too indolent to get rid, or inflated with conceit, will make little progress in understanding the facts of life. History teems with examples which teach us that candour of mind is rare, and that the tumultuous prejudices of mankind have postponed the advance of science and useful arts. The kingdom of knowledge belongs to the man of open mind. The single eye perceives what the double-minded man will never understand. Similarly, to the poor in spirit—to those whose souls are clear of the egotism of pride, indolence, self-sufficiency, self-indulgence—belongs the kingdom of God. God's kingdom is open to their eyes. The truth of that kingdom is theirs. To them it is a deep and unquestioned reality. They live in it. They feel that its order is round about their life. It enters into their thoughts. It governs their actions. It inspires their hearts.

Two thoughts arise here: (i.) One is that the

initial qualification of spiritual blessedness, according to our Lord, is the emptying of self. His first benediction is for the poor in spirit. Are we surprised at this? We shall hardly be when we remember that self lies at the root of sin. The tendency of self is to separate from the order of creation. It seeks to set up its own throne. It hearkens to the seductive promise, "Ye shall be as gods." It fondly believes that it can escape from the conditions of existence. It would find immunity from the pains and laws which visit other men. Its dream is to escape from its position as God's creature. It would fain be other than man; for its idea of greatness is to rise above its manhood. Here perverse wishes are accompanied by false thoughts. Perverse wishes show themselves in the desire to evade the laws of life which God has made. False thoughts are seen in the idea that there is greatness or dignity in doing so; for it is a mistake to suppose that greatness can be found in transcending our manhood. True greatness consists in fulfilling it, and the first step towards this greatness is the recognition of the wisdom of God. The fear or reverence of the Lord is the beginning of wisdom, said the wise man. This reverence will hardly be wise in its own conceit. It is content to find wisdom in believing in the divine wisdom. The thought of the wise man corresponds with the teaching of our Lord. The first step towards wisdom, like the first step towards happiness, is reverence for the divine order. To rule we must obey nature's powers. We must sit as docile pupils at the feet of God's universe and try to understand. Such is the first step towards wisdom, and the first step towards happiness is like to it. We must cease from self; we must learn self-dissatisfaction; we must be alive to our need, we must be self-emptied, poor in spirit. This step, which Christ points out as the first step on the pathway of happiness, is a step which He did not merely put before us as a command. He showed us the way by treading Himself that pathway of self-surrender. He showed us that human greatness was found in fulfilling our manhood, not in seeking to transcend it. He showed us that the way towards that fulfilment lay in the reverent and trustful acceptance of the divine will. The tempter suggested that He might escape privation by exercising more than human power (Matt. iv. 3), that He might set at naught the conditions of human existence and rely on heaven-sent help (Matt. iv. 6). But He showed that His life was to find its fulfilment in doing the Father's will as Son of Man, and not in any ostentatious disregard of the order of life. He showed us thus the way of life. He made Himself of no reputation. He became obedient to law for man. He lived the life of man with the spirit of a child of God; and He opened to us the kingdom of heaven when He said, "Except ye be converted and become as little children, ye shall not enter into the kingdom of heaven (Matt. xviii. 3). Blessed are the poor in spirit; for theirs is the kingdom of heaven."

(ii.) The second thought is this, that the blessings which Christ pronounces are not arbitrary blessings. When He says of the poor in spirit that theirs is the kingdom of God, He states what is in harmony with a natural order. The reward is not a capricious one. The reward is as a flower which rises from its root. The benediction springs out of the disposition. The kingdom of God does belong to the poor in spirit, and only the poor in spirit can possess it. There is sequence in the thought; there is a connection between the condition and the blessing. We have suggested this thought already. The kingdom of God does open upon the soul that is free from self. The unselfish, childlike spirit finds everywhere around him the realm of the heavenly Father.

A similar harmonious sequence is found in all the beatitudes. We are introduced to a kingdom, but it is a kingdom in which spiritual laws prevail.

The consolations of the soul of man arise out of the conditions of his soul. There is no heaven for unheavenly minds. The earthly mind may find the earthly reward and the worldly advantage. "They have their reward," our Lord said of the self-conscious pietists of His day. For the better reward there must be the better disposition; for the heavenly beatitude there must be the heavenly spirit. We see at once how all this turns the soul away from the baser gains and material advantages of life. The reward is spiritual. It is in the soul, and it is for the souls which are spiritual. If a man finds no attraction in the thought of an improved character, in spiritual progress, in a growing resemblance to God, there is for such a man no heaven. To be carnally minded is death; to be spiritually minded is life and peace (Rom. viii. 6).

Here we may reflect. We desire heaven. Yes; in moments of great peril or supreme excitement, or vivid realisation of that other world, we keenly desire heaven. At other times, we accept it as a sort of idle truism that all men hope for heaven. But do we desire heaven? Do we desire to be more full of goodness? Do we long to be just better men and better women—more pure-minded, more simply honest, more kind and gracious, more replete with the spirit of self-denial, more moved to a life whose motive is simple love? Then, but then only do we desire heaven, for to be such is to be in heaven; or rather to be such is to have reached that disposition which alone can perceive, live in, and rejoice in heaven. Other wishes—vague, selfish, indolent wishes, for a vacant happiness which means immunity from certain inconvenient and painful conditions—are not wishes for heaven, but for something else which probably is not heaven at all.

And this reflection may well bring us back to the earliest stage of conscious, religious life, even to Christ's first beatitude. Blessed indeed are those whose desires are free from impurity and misuse, who are poor in spirit, who have nothing of self in their thoughts. Blessed are they who can be as little children. Is the blessing far away out of our reach? Can we not become as little children, or has the world been too much with us? Has selfishness laid its strong hands upon us? Have we grown harder, more quick at over-passing our own desires, less scrupulous as to the method of attaining them? Is unselfishness of spirit impossible to us? Is the blessing out of our reach? Is the kingdom of heaven never to be ours? Never till the self disappears; never till the child-heart comes; never till we wish the wish and think the thought of

THE FIRST STEP TOWARDS HAPPINESS

God. Never? Impossible then to the old and hardened? Impossible! There is no irrevocableness with God. With Him all things are possible. To plunge into the river of His love is to get again the heart of a little child.

EVERY SEVERAL GATE WAS OF
ONE PEARL

Blessed are the poor in spirit : for their's is the kingdom of heaven.

Blessed are they that mourn : for they shall be comforted.

Blessed are the meek : for they shall inherit the earth.

Blessed are they which do hunger and thirst after righteousness : for they shall be filled.

Blessed are the merciful : for they shall obtain mercy.

Blessed are the pure in heart : for they shall see God.

Blessed are the peacemakers ; for they shall be called the children of God.-

Blessed are they which are persecuted for righteousness' sake : for their's is the kingdom of heaven.

Blessed are ye, when men shall revile you, and persecute you, and shall say all manner of evil against you falsely, for my sake.

Rejoice, and be exceeding glad : for great is your reward in heaven : for so persecuted they the prophets which were before you.

EVERY SEVERAL GATE WAS OF ONE PEARL

THE beatitudes have been likened to a string of pearls. The comparison is just; for each beatitude like each pearl has its own special and peculiar beauty.

1. The first pearl on the string is—*Blessed are the poor in spirit; for theirs is the kingdom of heaven.* We have dwelt upon this beatitude at some length. It was needful; for on the true understanding of this benediction much depends. It is our Lord's first blessing. This He sets forth before all others as the leading benediction of His kingdom. The temper of soul expressed by the words "poor in spirit" is indispensable. Without it there is no possession of the heavenly kingdom. Without it any quantity of earthly things may be ours—acres of land, houses full of silver and gold, the decorations of worldly honour and the plaudits of men, but not one rood of territory in the divine kingdom.

But he who is poor in spirit, though he may own no whit of the earthly possessions, yet owns, not one rood only of heaven, but the whole of that kingdom. There is no spot in the divine realm which is not his who is poor in spirit. He claims nothing as his own, and therefore all things are his. He has ceased from self. He lives by love and for love; and so all earth and heaven and all deep places are his. "Pauper est," says Bengel sweetly, "qui non habet dicere, hoc meum est." He is poor who has it not in his power to say, "This is mine." He depends upon another—that is, God. He is poor who looks to God for all and claims nothing as his own, save the right to serve others by love.

The spirit of this first blessing lives in all the beatitudes. The disposition which is needful for the possession of the kingdom of God is needful for the inheritance of all the blessings of that kingdom. The first beatitude is the portal to all the rest.

II. *Blessed are the meek; for they shall inherit the earth.*

The verses should be inverted. The benediction of the meek should follow immediately on the blessing of the poor in spirit. And this because the two dispositions are so allied that one may be said to grow out of the other. The meekness which is blessed is the offspring of poverty of spirit. It is the next rung of the Christian ladder. The poor in spirit may step onward to meekness, which none can reach save those who are already poor in spirit. And as the dispositions are allied to one another, so also the blessings which wait upon them are related. The possession of the poor in spirit is the kingdom of heaven. The inheritance of the meek is the earth.

Who then are the meek, who thus shall inherit the earth? Here we must beware, as in the case of the previous beatitude, of degrading or perverting the meaning of the word meekness. It is a disposition which Christ singles out as a blessed and happy one, and which He declares to be full of a singular mightiness, so great and forceful in its nature that it will in the end inherit the earth.

And first let us note that it is not to be mistaken for weakness, any more than poverty of spirit is to be identified with mean-spiritedness.

Meekness, in the judgment of Aristotle, is a kind of propriety of affection in matters which provoke anger. It holds a middle place between irascibility and that indifference or incapacity of feeling which can never be roused to wrath. The meek man can be angry on fit occasions, but he holds his passion in control and will not be surprised into wrath His spirit is free from the perturbations which easily stirred souls experience. Thus the meek man, though moved by anger on righteous occasions, yet inclines to a defective extreme; since he is not resentful of injuries, but always prone to pardon them. And this inability to feel just provocation is a fault, denoting a stupid insensibility of character.

It will be seen that the philosopher's idea of meekness falls behind the Christian idea. With the philosopher the meekness proceeds from dulness and insensibility. It is a defect of nature, and not a victory over it. In our Lord's lips the idea of meekness is a much richer and rarer one than this. It has strength where the ancient only saw weakness. It is not irascible, because it is lord of itself. It is not vindictive because possessed of larger thoughts; the injuries of life are of less moment than they would be to lesser men. It is closely allied to the lowliness of mind or poverty of spirit which possesses heaven; and on the other side it is linked with that reticence and self-control of nature which belong to strong characters or rather to those to whom heaven's inward strength has come. "It is," said Archbishop Trench, "not in a man's outward behaviour only; nor yet in his relations to his fellow-men; as little in his mere natural disposition. Rather is it an inwrought grace of the soul; and the exercises of it are first and chiefly towards God" (Matt. xi. 29; James i. 21). It is that temper of spirit in which we accept His dealings with us as good, and therefore without disputing or resisting.* Much of this is true and well said; and in a sense the chief exercise of meekness is indeed towards God. But in the beatitudes, it is not this feature, I think, which is given prominence.

The two beatitudes of poverty of spirit and meekness are linked together; but the first looks out towards heaven, the second by comparison has its glance towards the earth. The poverty of spirit implies that upward look which is the impulse of one who has first looked within and found how empty and barren he is in himself, who has found that all is from above, and who, ceasing from self, longs to be filled with the fulness of God. Meekness looks out upon the earth with large and God-filled soul, and moves forward to the conquest of the earth with the patient, strong, self-restrained spirit of one who has learned that all is of God, and that to Him belong the earth and the sea and all deep places, and who therefore endures with gentleness and patience the buffets of the world; as the sailor meets the lashing of the waves, when he knows that his vessel is strong, his pilot skilful, and his entry into port certain. In poverty of spirit we have the upward glance of the soul which

* "Synonyms of the New Testament," p. 144.

has found all in God and nothing in self. In meekness we have the glance of the same soul towards the world when it has taken another step and is advancing towards earth as its sphere of duty, in the strength of God.

And this is the spirit which possesses the earth. The most superficial view of life may well warn us that the quality which Aristotle opposed to meekness will hardly win the world. The irascible man conquers nothing, for the simple reason that he who has not conquered himself is foredoomed to failure sooner or later. Meekness, as far as it implies a glorious sovereignty over self, is a victorious quality; for it is the staying power which means patience and endurance, and is assured of the spoil which belongs to those who can wait.* The truth of this will become more apparent from day to day, for it is even now being brought home to men that the true inheritance of the earth does not consist in those material conquests which dazzled the ambitions of worldly heroes, but in the mastery of those laws and principles by which all things are governed. He who knows a law of nature and can apply it has a

---

* Keim says that those here blessed are not the meek but the poor (*e.g.*, Psalms xxxvii. 11), who, in contrast with the high-minded sinners, wait *upon the Lord*. He translates; "Blessed are those that wait (die Harrenden)."

truer inheritance in the earth than he who has won a battle and annexed a territory. And he whose life is animated by the Spirit of God has a nobler inheritance than either. "Pyramids, arches, obelisks," wrote Sir Thomas Browne, "were but the irregularities of vain glory, and wild enormities of ancient magnanimity. But the most magnanimous resolution rests in the Christian religion, which trampleth upon pride and sits on the neck of ambition, humbly pursuing that infallible perpetuity unto which all others diminish their diameters." (Urn-Burial.)

III. *Blessed are they that mourn; for they shall be comforted.*

And this after all is the most wonderful of beatitudes; for here is a most strange paradox, that there should be happiness in that which denies all happiness, and blessing in mourning. And yet there is no truer beatitude than this. For we may view the world as the world of sin, wherein many, vanquished by passion and temptation, have fallen into strengthlessness and despair; or we may see it as a world wherein men are moving forward from epoch to epoch, to an ever higher and yet higher goal. And in whichever way we look at the world we shall see the benediction of sorrow. For if the world be the world of men who fall because of sin, he cannot have a blessed or happy heart who mourns not over what he sees and what he feels; and if the world be the place wherein loftier heights beckon us to climb ever upward, he cannot be blessed who is content where he is and knows no mourning for the heights which he has failed to win. In the one case, inability to mourn shows lack of sympathy: in the other, it shows an ignominious contentment, and lack of that ideal which teaches us our shortcomings and spurs us to fresh endeavour. In both cases it argues a lack of self-knowledge, and is therefore a lack of unhappiness which is most unhappy.

And the saying has a message for the distressed and troubled. It is not only the sympathetic mourner for the sorrows and sins of the world, nor the ardent soul striving to reach loftier altitudes of virtue, who are remembered in this beatitude. It spreads the skirts of its blessing wider, even over those who are in any trouble, need, sickness, or adversity. To such there is a message. These contrarieties of life are not meaningless or valueless. They are part of the discipline and education of life: they bring forth hereafter the peaceable fruit of righteousness to those who are exercised thereby (Heb. xii. 11): they enable the afflicted to make manifest the higher works of God in the triumph of patience and sweetness in the midst of trouble (John ix. 3). Comfort is promised to these; and the comfort will be theirs in the future (*cf.* Luke xvi. 25) when the meaning of all things will be made clear; yet even here and now they know consolation inasmuch as they can glory in tribulation, knowing that tribulation worketh patience, and patience experience, and experience hope (Rom. v. 3–5). Men can value the sorrow which gives them the opportunity of testing and proving the principles of the inward life. They can count it all joy when they fall into diverse temptations, knowing that the trial of faith worketh patience (James i. 3). The heathen world perceived in a measure this truth of the inward value of affliction. The brave man, according to Seneca, regarded adversities as exercises; and nothing was more unhappy than that a man should meet with nothing adverse, for such a one had no chance of putting himself to the proof. In the knowledge of these benefits to character arising out of affliction, there is comfort; but it is only assured comfort to those who know that the trials of life are meted out by that wise love which chastens only for our profit, that we might be partakers of His holiness (Heb. xii. 10) and doth not afflict willingly the children of men (Lam. iii. 33).

And if in no other way there were comfort in trial, yet there is in this (and it is eminently a Christian aspect of sorrow) that we gather an experience which makes us skilful and tender in ministering to others when in sorrow. There are few nobler sayings than that of the apostle, when he taught this truth to the Corinthians (2 Cor. i. 3, 4) and told them of the God of comfort, who comforteth us in all our tribulation, that we may be able to comfort them which are in any trouble by the comfort wherewith we ourselves are comforted of God. Thus does St. Paul speak of that solidarity of love which through the instrumentality of sorrow binds man to man by binding man to God. Nor need we be surprised who know that the Man of Sorrows is the Prince of comfort and of peace. So sure and certain is the beatitude—"Blessed are they that mourn; for they shall be comforted."

IV. *Blessed are they that hunger and thirst after righteousness; for they shall be filled.*

This beatitude adds a sense of vigour to those which have gone before, and in so doing prepares us for the more active beatitude which follows; for though lowliness of mind, meek patience, and deep sorrowfulness are blessings inasmuch as they indicate a spirit not dead but alive, yet they suggest qualities which are somewhat negative in character, were there not added to them the strong, vigorous, passionate longing for some real positive force like righteousness. And this strong desire Christ expresses by the images of hunger and thirst. In this He uses images which were familiar to those who read the Old Testament. The Psalmist had described his desire after God as a great and unsatisfied thirst—"My soul thirsteth for Thee, my flesh longeth for Thee in a dry and thirsty land where no water is" (Ps. lxiii. 1). "As the hart panteth after the water brooks, so panteth my soul after Thee, O God. My soul thirsteth for God, for the living God." And almost as if in answer to this great cry of thirst the great prophet proclaims the freely given water (Ps. xlii. 1, 2). "Ho, every one that thirsteth, come ye to the waters, and he that hath no money; come ye, buy, and eat; yea, come, buy wine and milk without money and without price" (Isa. lv. 1). The image expresses the truth that there is something which the soul of man feels to be necessary to its very life. He must eat of the tree which can give him life (Gen. iii. 22–24). There is a divine food which is essential to the human life. It is the sense that food and drink are needful for existence which gives such acuteness to hunger and thirst. How happy, says Jesus Christ, are they who have found that righteousness is indispensable to their life. Happy, indeed! for it is a tremendous discovery, and it is by no means a world-wide one. The saddest, maddest spectacle of the world's sorrow is this—that thousands upon thousands do not feel that righteousness is necessary to their life. They have a vague idea that they ought to be good and some transient wishes that they might be so; but these thin and spasmodic emotions are very far removed from the state of soul which feels that it must have righteousness with the same intensity that a starving man feels that he must have food. The weak and passing wishes after goodness lead to no determined effort. The passion for what is felt to be necessary will spare no effort and take no denial. It is urged onwards by that necessity which is the spur to vigour as well as the mother of invention. Here the attitude, then, is very different from that of the meek and waiting soul. Here is the spirit of that violence which taketh the kingdom of God by force (Matt. xi. 12). Here is the spirit of the glorious wrestler who cries, "I will not let thee go except thou bless me" (Gen. xxxii. 26).

It is not in the very earliest stages of the religious life that we truly discover this or experience this holy hunger and thirst. We need to have climbed the earlier rungs of the ladder before we reach this one. Pride and self-satisfaction must have been banished: the soul must have waited on God and mourned over evil, before it can fully and vividly realise that righteousness is indeed the very necessity of life. But when this stage is reached, it is in a new region of happiness; for it is ever a blessed thing to know truly and really what we need. Half human life (ah! more than half) is spent in desiring we know not what. We scarcely know what we wish or we wish for things which cannot possibly satisfy our desire, but which we fondly imagine will do so. In countless experiences and manifold merciful ways, the voice of divine love cries in pity. "Whoso drinketh of this water will thirst again" (John iv. 13). "Wherefore do ye spend your money for that which is not bread, and your labour for that which satisfieth not?" (Is. lv. 2).

Without righteousness there is no satisfaction for moral beings; and the righteousness which can satisfy is not a righteousness before man, or a righteousness which reaches to the level of society's expectations. The righteousness hungered for must be a real and true righteousness, even a righteousness of the soul itself.

"Non significatur hic jus fori humani, sed divini. ... Non dicit, beati justi, ut mox dicit, beati misericordes, &c., sed, esurientes et sitientes justitiam" (Bengel). The righteousness is not a righteousness which will meet conventional requirements. That which is desired is a righteousness which is felt to be necessary and is known to be out of reach; and is therefore hungered and thirsted for with a desire which cannot be satisfied with any lower thing.

> " La sete natural che mai non sazia
> Se non con l'acqua onde la femminetta
> Samaritana domandò la grazia." *

The food must be divine which each new-born soul desires. It is true, real inward righteousness, exceeding that of Scribes and Pharisees, which the spirit requires. To be offered anything else is to ask bread and to be given a stone.

And what is the reward? Those so hungering and thirsting shall be filled. With what? With the happiness of Messiah's kingdom? With the splendours and authorities of heaven? No; but with that which they have desired. They hungered for righteousness—with righteousness shall they be filled. They thirsted for righteousness—with the gift of righteousness shall they be satisfied. They shall be that which they desired to be. They shall be righteous. They shall be called, "Trees of righteousness, the planting of the Lord" (Is. lxi. 3). They shall be covered with the robe of righteousness—not a fictitious, but a real righteousness (Is. lxi. 10); for they will wake up after God's likeness and be satisfied with it (Ps. xvii. 15). Here and now they grow from strength to strength amid many

* "Purg." xxi. 1–3.

difficulties and with much failing. The future is dark. "They know not what they shall be;" but the future blessedness for which they hunger is certain; "for they shall be like Him, for they shall see Him as He is" (1 John iii. 2).

v. *Blessed are the merciful; for they shall obtain mercy.*

It has sometimes been objected that the Christian ideal is too negative. It applauds the virtues of resignation, meekness, and passive endurance; but it has little to say of the more sturdy and active virtues. It lacks virility. The charge is not true, though some facts may make it seem true to certain minds. It is a fact that Jesus Christ discouraged violence and roughness, and anything approaching to arrogant self-assertion. Strength was to be used, but chivalrously, not rudely, with a noble self-mastery and a wise thoughtfulness for others, and in no way selfishly. And men have been ready to admit this principle ever since the time when they began to aspire to be gentlemen. Yet no one thinks that in being a gentleman, a man loses anything of his virility or proper manhood. It is rather felt that in sweet courtesy and easy self-restraint, manhood is becoming more truly manly, it being no part of manliness to be the slave of the impulses of pride or passion, of petulance or greed. It follows that in placing lowliness, meekness and gentleness before men, Christ did not lower the dignity of man, but raised it to a higher level. But neither did our Lord so raise and refine it that the vigorous forces of manhood were lost sight of. He does not inculcate passive virtues only. Human happiness could not be so found, for man's nature is active. His bliss is only found in being up and doing. The limit of this vigour was given in the last beatitude. The hunger and thirst for righteousness must prompt to earnest action. But it is in the present beatitude that the active virtues are first completely and definitely expressed. Happiness is found in mercy; and Mercy, once she looks out upon the world, finds ceaseless employment. She may be ever working; for deeds of mercy may be daily, hourly, continuously done.

And here let it be noted that the virtues which bring happiness take on a most divine hue. The earlier beatitudes are in a sense, as Keim describes them, virtues of sorrow. We feel that the touch of human weakness and frailty is more or less upon them. But in being merciful, men rise above themselves, and become most divine indeed, being then most like to Him whose tender mercy is over all His works. Then, too, they rise above the level of a mere earthly wisdom: they live in the atmosphere of that wisdom from above, one of whose characteristics it is to be full of mercy, and that of an active sort, for it is also full of good works (James iii. 17).

But the reminder that we are but men remains in the beatitude, notwithstanding the height of heavenly bliss to which it lifts us; for the blessing which waits upon the merciful calls back the remembrance of our frailty and of our falls, and promises that mercy which the very best of us must stand in need of; for the promise to the merciful is, "they shall obtain mercy." Thus sweetly and wisely does our Lord lift us to heaven, and lower us to earth, that we may know ourselves even when we know God, and in knowing God, know both what He would have us do and what He will do for us. "Mercy, misericordia," says Ruskin, "does not in the least mean forgiveness of sins, but pity of sorrows." And this indeed is true; but yet, seeing there is no sorrow like the sorrow which the sense of sins brings, it is the divine pity for such sorrow which brings the forgiveness of sins; but even this (so we are taught) would never come to the man of merciless heart. He who had no pity for his fellow-servant, should look for no pity from his lord (Matt. xxv. 41-46); for the divine mercy cannot have entered his heart who shuts up his heart against his brother's need (1 John iii. 17). Thus, as Quarles says, "Mercy turns her back upon the unmerciful." And here we see again how all happiness just means likeness to God. The happiness of heaven cannot be his whose hard and merciless heart knows no pity, melts at no distress and beats with no sympathy for others. It is he whose heart is full of a sort of divine mercifulness who knows the happiness of heaven. In howsoever small a degree we reflect the character of God we catch the light of heaven's bliss, and yet it is chiefly through God's dear mercy known that we awaken to the joy of such mercifulness of spirit.

> " To threats the stubborn sinner oft is hard
> Wrapped in his crimes, against the storm prepared;
> But when the milder beams of mercy play,
> He melts, and throws his cumbrous cloak away.'

And thus both these things are true. It is through the exercise of mercifulness that we find God's mercy. It is the mercy of God which inspires our mercifulness. It is the story of the mirror and the light again. It is through the light on the mirror that we know that there is light elsewhere; and it is because the light shines that the mirror can reflect the light. Our mercifulness but reflects God's mercy, and our mercifulness is the assurance that there is mercy with God. We know His mercy through our own, because our own is but the shadow of His. So, "blessed are the merciful; for they shall obtain mercy."

VI. *Blessed are the pure in heart; for they shall see God.*

In this beatitude, as in all His teaching, our Lord does more than merely promise a specific blessing to a specific virtue. He affirms a principle of the spiritual kingdom. The principle is the never-to-be-forgotten one, that our powers of perception are narrowed or enlarged by our moral condition. This is no new principle; for it belongs to the eternal order of God. Neither is it a newly stated principle, for it had been enunciated in Old Testament times. The writer of the 50th Psalm glanced at this truth when he showed that God wanted no sacrifice but that of thanksgiving, and no honour but that of a true life, and declared that to such the revelation of God would be made known. "To him that ordereth his conversation aright will I show the salvation of God" (Ps. l. 23). A similar thought was in the words of David, "With the pure thou shalt be pure" (2 Sam. xxii. 27; *cf.* Ps. xviii. 26). It is found again with a difference in Is. lxvi. 2: "To this man will I look, even to him that is poor and of a contrite spirit." All these passages are united by the common principle that the vision of God to the soul is conditioned by the state of the heart. It is this which Christ once more affirms. The heart must be pure. The foolish heart is darkened (Rom. i. 21). The single-minded has light (Matt. vi. 22). "A pure heart penetrateth heaven and hell," said the author of the "Imitation."

And similar is the thought which Tennyson put into the mouth of Sir Galahad:

> "More bounteous aspects on me beam,
>   Me mightier transports move and thrill;
> So keep I fair thro' faith and prayer
>   A virgin heart in work and will."

For this purity which Christ declares to be blessed is not purity in one matter alone. It is not the purity of the Pharisee who thought chiefly of ceremonial purity. Epictetus took a higher view of purity than this, for he said, "The highest purity is that which is in the soul" (Bk. iv. ch. 11). With a word Christ cuts off all thought of mere outward purity. He does not say, "Blessed are the ceremonially clean"; for He saw that there were many who made clean the outside of the cup and platter, but within were full of extortion and excess. Such He counselled to cleanse that which is within (Matt. xxiii. 25, 26). So with a word here He keeps that inward cleanness before His disciples, for He says, "Blessed are the pure in heart." And in doing this, He asks a more real purity than that of the body merely. He asks that the thoughts of the heart may be pure also. He tells us that wandering desires dim the vision of God to the soul. He tells us that doubtful or selfish motives mingling with our good deeds, defile them. He asks no less the purity of a single eye than the chastity of the heart. "Purity of heart," says Bengel rightly, "embraces chastity and freedom from the other defilements of sin." Hypocrisy and worldliness of spirit is excluded; for we must keep those interpreting words of Christ Himself, "Thou hast hid these things from the wise and prudent, and hast revealed them unto babes" (Luke x. 21). The purity includes the simplicity, directness, singlemindedness, and unselfishness of the child just as it excludes those lower and animal passions which degrade the body, defile the soul, and spread grossness over the mind.

The blessing is, They shall see God. No doubt in the hereafter, when the disciplining work of God is completed and when we are like Him, we shall see Him as He is; but even here and now, insight is the portion of the pure in heart. For the jaded sensualist sees nothing of the beauty which is open to other and purer eyes. "The luxurious soul," said St. Chrysostom, "is unable to hear or see anything." On the other hand, it has been well said of the pure in heart: "Isti sunt præ ceteris capaces cognitionis Dei, ut enim oculo tenebræ, ita cordi peccatorum sordes officiunt quoad visionem Dei." Such are, more than others, fit for the knowledge of God; for as darkness hinders the eye, so doth the filth of sins hinder the heart in the vision of God. God's judgments are to the soul immersed in sin, as the Psalmist said, far above out of his sight (Ps. x. 5). But to the pure, the ways of the Lord are right, the laws of the Lord are good. And the hill of the Lord, on whose summit all light shines, is no inaccessible height. Who shall ascend the hill of the Lord? He that hath clean hands and a pure heart (Ps. xxiv. 3, 4). As the full vision of God belongs hereafter to the pure in heart, for without holiness no man shall see the Lord (Heb. xii. 14), so in the present, the way of life below is happier, for such gain glimpses of His love, and read tokens of His presence unnoted of other men. They know that fuller disclosures of His character await them. So blessed in fruition and in hope are the pure in heart, who in a sense now see, and hereafter shall more fully see, God.

VII. *Blessed are the peacemakers; for they shall be called the children of God.*

The next feature of those who belong to the blessed kingdom of God is that they are peacemaking. Some have taken the word peacemakers as though it meant simply men of a peaceable disposition. It is quite true that this peaceable temper will almost certainly belong to the peacemaker. We may almost say that such a temper is indispensable for successful peacemaking, and we might almost say that Christ takes this for granted, since He has just said that the pure in heart shall see God; and this inward purity with its accompanying blessing of the near realisation of God's presence can hardly fail to promote that inward moral harmony and calm disposition which create the peaceable spirit. But to limit the thought of Christ to this inner peacefulness is to miss much of the meaning and fulness of the beatitude. It must be kept in mind, moreover, that in the second portion of the beatitudes we pass into the active and positive spheres of heavenly blessing. The earlier beatitudes are more negative in character. After the central one (Blessed are they that hunger and thirst after righteousness) we pass into the region of activity. We see the outstretched hand of active mercy: we hear the revelation of the Divine Presence, which only the pure-hearted can disclose; and in our present beatitude we see the active force of those who do not simply enjoy peace, but seek in every possible form to promote peace. Those whom Christ declares to be blessed are those who, being themselves at peace, seek to make peace everywhere and at all times. They will strive to make men of one mind in a house. They will seek to make them realise the brotherhood of man. They will promote peace wherever there has been quarrel or dissension. They will be mindful not to let the sun go down upon their wrath (Eph. iv. 26). They will seek to reconcile the offended, to do good to their enemies (Rom. xii. 20; Matt. v. 44), to make peace between foes, to bring all men into peace with one another and with God.

They will strive to reconcile man with man and man with God. They will follow peace with all men (Heb. xii. 14). They will seek peace and ensue it (1 Pet. iii. 11), and in doing this they will achieve something greater than the mere possession of a peaceful heart, or a life untroubled with conflict; for as Dean Plumptre truly wrote: "To be able to say with power to those who are bitter foes, 'Sirs, ye are brethren' (Acts vii. 26) is nobler even than to strive to live peaceably with all men (Rom. xii. 18)." Yes, nobler indeed; for to secure peace for ourselves in our souls or in our circumstances is not so noble as to promote true peace among men; for this latter involves, perchance, the sacrifice of the personal tranquillity which is so dear to peaceable dispositions. Was not Moses himself an example of this, who brought trouble on himself in seeking to make peace among his brethren (Exod. ii. 13–15)? And does not our Lord give the hint of this, when He passes immediately from the benediction of the peacemaker to the blessing of those who are persecuted for righteousness' sake? Nay, does not the reward which He promises to the peacemaker carry a hint of the same thing?

They shall be called the children (rather, the sons) of God. Whatever they aspire to, they cannot aspire to higher than this, to be called like their Master, sons of God. And must not those who are thus named be prepared to drink the cup of which He drank (Matt. xx. 22), and to find, like their Lord when they labour for peace, there are those who make them ready for battle (Ps. cxx. 7)?

But their reward is sure, and it is high. They shall be called the sons of God; and this because they show in deed the spirit of their Father, who is the God of peace (Rom. xvi. 20), and because they follow the example of their Master, who as Son of God was also Prince of Peace (Is. ix, 6), and made peace and proclaimed peace on earth (Col. i. 20; Eph. ii. 14; Luke ii. 14). The name given to them will be no empty name, no idle and ostentatious apotheosis. It will be the name given to those who are called sons of God, because their spirit and life reveal that they are sons of God. The world will take knowledge of them, and recognise what they truly are. And this is no small thing, that a man should so live that the world, though perchance persecuting him and saying all manner of evil against him, should nevertheless acknowledge that the life he lived had in it something of heaven, and should confess that he was on the earth like a son of God. To have so wrought upon the heart and conscience of mankind is not to have lived in vain, and is to be happy indeed. And such is the happiness of this beatitude. "Blessed are the peacemakers; for they shall be called the sons of God."

VIII. *Blessed are they that are persecuted for righteousness' sake; for theirs is the kingdom of heaven.*

The blessings in the previous beatitudes belonged to a certain disposition or character. This last pronounces a blessing on those whose character endures in the time of testing. It is blessed to have a certain character, but the reality of the blessing and of the character, is brought out in the time of trial. Thus, this eighth beatitude sets the seal upon the seven which precede. It is not a distinct beatitude, as it were; it adds to the others no new inward quality. It only says blessed are they who, possessing the love of righteousness, can stand the ordeal which tests reality. The inward love of righteousness is assumed. It is not persecution which makes a saint. It is the love of righteousness which transforms the sufferer into the saintly sufferer. And here it is to be noted that it is the love of righteousness which, in Christ's view, is the indispensable condition of the beatitude. It is righteousness, neither more nor less than living and active righteousness, which our Lord has in view.

It includes a keen sense of justice. The Latin versions remind us of this. Blessed are they that are persecuted for the sake of justice (*propter justitiam*—Old Version—*justitiæ causa*—Beza). A man may be a martyr for his own opinions. In this case we may justly condemn his persecutors without in any way approving his opinions. And, broadly speaking, the opinions for which he suffers do not make him a sufferer for righteousness' sake. The martyr for opinion's sake is chiefly a martyr in this, that he will not, for fear or favour, utter an untruth or declare himself a believer of that which he does not believe. It is his loyalty to his own conviction and conscience which makes him a sufferer for righteousness' sake—rather than the special opinions true or false which he holds. This distinction is necessary if we are to be fair towards men whose opinions we do not share. It may be paradox but it is true, that a man who holds mistaken views and suffers for his honesty may be truly a sufferer for righteousness' sake, while the most scrupulous orthodoxy may miss the benediction. The ethical attitude of the man may be right while his opinions may be wrong. And the ethical attitude of orthodoxy may be wholly unrighteous. Dr. Döllinger pointed out that the want of justice was called by men fanaticism and that there have been times when the best of men have acted fanatically—*i.e.*, without justice. When Philip Augustus robbed and exiled the Jews, the Pope declared that he had acted out of godly zeal. Even holy Ambrose "pronounced the burning of a Synagogue in Rome to be a deed well-pleasing to God." In the view of Christ the benediction falls on those whose hearts are set on righteousness. In the quarrels and persecutions which have been waged in the name of religion, the blessing of Christ must often have fallen, not on those who were most stalwart for true opinions, but on the man, mistaken yet honest in his error, who would not pretend a faith which was not his, nor make his judgment blind. In this, he must be truthful. Truthfulness is justice to conviction. It is better to be honestly wrong than dishonestly right; for then the man is right though his views may be wrong. It is best of all to be both right and honest; but it is indispensable that a man be honest. Then, if persecuted, he is persecuted for righteousness' sake. To win this blessing, it is needful that a man should hunger and thirst for righteousness. He must see that the cause of right can never be advanced by ways that are not right. The kingdom of heaven can never be won by the man who seeks to establish it by the violation of the laws of that kingdom. "Theirs is the kingdom of heaven" is the promise to those who hold fast their righteousness in spite of every opposition, and who can cling loyally to the laws of God, even when the professed servants of God cast them out as evil and pronounce them heretic.

Theirs is the kingdom of heaven. Not often, indeed, have such men won the kingdom of earth. The recognition of the wide application of the law of righteousness is rare. Few can do justice toward those who differ from them. The weight of the ruling opinion presses hard upon the man who declares for righteousness against privilege and against accepted maxims. But there are glimpses of heaven for the courageous souls who have followed righteousness at all hazards. "I separate thee from God's Church on earth," shouted the persecutors of Savonarola. "But not from the

Church in heaven," answered the lonely hero. Theirs is the kingdom of heaven. Can we not see that it must be so? The follower of righteousness has grasped the laws of the kingdom. He who lives under the laws of any realm has gone far towards enjoying its blessings. He who has suffered rather than renounce the righteous order of God's kingdom, has already tasted of its glory.

KNOWN AND UNKNOWN INFLUENCE

Ye are the salt of the earth : but if the salt have lost his savour, wherewith shall it be salted? it is thenceforth good for nothing, but to be cast out, and to be trodden under foot of men.

Ye are the light of the world. A city that is set on an hill cannot be hid.

Neither do men light a candle, and put it under a bushel, but on a candlestick ; and it giveth light unto all that are in the house.

Let your light so shine before men, that they may see your good works, and glorify your Father which is in heaven.

KNOWN AND UNKNOWN INFLUENCE

HAPPINESS is not found in the acquisition of wealth, or in the proud consciousness of human applause. It is found rather in the possession of right dispositions and in the living of a life in harmony with them. It lies not in material things, but rather in living according to the order of our being. It is found in the realisation of our true place in God's world; and in using our capacities there for the good of the world. Riches, possessions, applause are powerless to bless. But the poor in spirit, the meek, the pure-hearted, the earnest striver after righteousness or the patient sufferer for it—these and such as these are blessed.

So our Lord taught in His beatitudes. The excitement, cares and apprehensions of existence hung over the hearts of those to whom He spoke. The fever of life was in their veins. False dreams of happiness filled their imaginations, as they have filled ours. A little mitigation of the severity of their lot, a little kindlier atmosphere around them—just a little more than was theirs already, and happiness would seem to be within their grasp. But from these vain dreamings our Lord turned away their thoughts. He led them into calmer and serener air. The breezes round them were healthier and more invigorating than those which met them in the dreamland of their ambitions and their cares. He told them that they possessed capacities for happiness which they had hardly used and which they little realised. In the exercise of their inward faculties, in the cultivation of better dispositions, in the freer working of these deep impulses towards good which had been checked and neglected, in realising the joy of growing to be better men, they might find a gladness which had escaped them hitherto. He told them of unfathomed depths of joy and higher capacities of happiness than they had ever known. Thus He sought to detach them from the grasp of the world, from the tyrannous passion of acquisition, from the melancholy power of discontent. He told them that there was work before them which was worthy of their ambition. He assured them that they might be powers in the world. He pointed to their capacities, and urged them to turn them to use: "Ye are the salt of the earth. Ye are the light of the world."

Thus from the conditions of happiness, He passes to the duties of usefulness. From the beatitudes, He points to the range of human influence. And naturally so, for man is so made that his happiness is not possible except in exertion. As the universe teaches not simply eternal being, but an eternal becoming; so man cannot find rest in stagnation, but in the congenial exercise of his powers. He cannot be happy in the mere possession of capacity. He needs to use it. This capacity our Lord speaks of under two emblems, light and salt: "Ye are the salt of the earth. Ye are the light of the world."

We can see the appropriateness of the imagery. For the virtue and value of both light and salt are in their diffusive power; the one spreading illumination and the other health. The one enlightening: the other preserving.

1. Let us invert the order, and take first the more usual emblem—*light:* "Ye are the light of the world."

The meaning is simple. We grasp it best perhaps by recalling the men who have shone as lights in the world. We must think not so much of the splendour which invests the names of men like Socrates and Plato, Solon and Lycurgus, Newton and Harvey, as of the light which these in their various ways cast upon human life—enlarging the range of knowledge, clearing what was obscure; revealing order where before there was but chaos. From these men there streamed beams which brightened the earth and made the pathway of men clearer and safer. We can see that the influence of these men was the result of a determined, vigorous, and systematic concentration of their powers upon one object. The quality of their influence as light was the possession of a certain definite message or truth for men and the energy to express it. Conscious vigour directed their action. Thought and force combined to disclose and to diffuse light among men.

But men such as these are not the only luminaries of the world. The light which spread from these men was mainly light in intellectual matters. From them came the vigorous thought which forced its way into untrodden realms, and enlarged the empire of human knowledge by the annexation of fresh kingdoms. But there have been lights of another sort. There have been men who shed light upon the moral life of mankind. Besides philosophers like Aristotle and discoverers like Galileo, there have been prophets like Moses and Elijah, like John the Baptist and Savonarola. From these have radiated a light which has penetrated the consciences of men, and has brought realms of human nature under the sovereignty of moral influence. This light, seeing that it is ethical, comes with even greater energy than mere intellectual light. Such men are not merely lights, they are, as our Lord described John the Baptist, burning and shining lights. The beams which spread from them pierce into recesses of the human heart which Plato and Bacon were powerless to reach.

Now a power of this kind Christ claims on the part of all His followers. When He says " Ye are the light of the world," He means that there is in every man the capacity to be a light in his day. As men of greatness have by vigour and concentration spread their influence in the world, so may every man, who will bend his mind and will to the matter, become the bearer of some message to his brother men. Light clear, distinct and encouraging, may shine from every human life, and may make the pathway of a brother-man clearer and easier. It is true that it is not given to every man to make fresh discoveries, but every man may be a witness to the moral order of the universe, to the true grounds of happiness, to the responsibility of life.

And here let no one say that all cannot be lights, because all cannot be great. The brilliancy of the lights may differ as one star differeth from another star in glory, but all may shine as lights in the world. The brilliancy of the light depends upon the quality or quantity of the stuff composing the candle; but the question is not of the splendour of the candle when lighted, but of the fact whether it is alight or not. Some men have qualities and capacities which may make them apostles, evangelists, doctors and pastors. They have their gifts, one after this manner, another after that. The range of their influence may be in proportion to their gifts, just as the circle of light from the candle may be smaller or larger. But the range of possible influence is one thing: the exertion of whatever influence we may possess is another. Indeed, usefulness is not identical with brilliancy. The farthing candle has been enough to light the philosopher as he penned his deathless treatise, while splendid lights have often only lighted men through gaiety to death. What our Lord insists on is that men are capable of diffusing light. It is possible to make the life shed a steady and unmistakable light among men. The quality may not be the richest, the quantity may be scant, but if the taper be lighted, the duty which God asks has been done. The foolish virgins were not blamed because the light they carried was feeble, but because they allowed their lamps to go out. Therefore Christ says to all—" Let your light shine. Let it be placed where it can be seen." " Neither do men light a lamp and put it under the bushel, but on the stand; and it shineth unto all that are in the house."

The powers of life are to be used. The influence we possess should be felt.

"If our virtues did not go forth of us, 'twere all alike as if we had them not." We must not be passive spectators, but active agents in life. We must consciously and deliberately do all we can to diffuse in the world the light of juster conceptions of God, of life, and of duty. Our will, strength, and intelligence should be enlisted in making religion a felt power, that by character and conduct we may shine as lights in the world.

II. But Christ also said, "Ye are the salt of the earth." There is a resemblance between the two emblems—light and salt. Both are useful. The one illuminates; the other preserves. Both make their usefulness operative by diffusion of their powers. But they offer contrasts as well as resemblances; for the power which renders the candle useful is the light which is communicated to it from without, while the power which makes the salt useful is the quality of saltness which belongs to it by nature. The one acts by an acquired force, the other by an inherent power. Further, in process of time, the candle wastes away; as the light burns the substance of the candle vanishes. Its outward form perishes. The disappearance of the light is one with the wasting of its substance. But with salt the quality may disappear while the substance remains. The outward appearance may be just what it was at the first, but the virtue may have gone from it. The salt may be there, but the saltness may have passed out of it.

The influence of light is clear, unmistakable; it displays itself by its own light; it can be seen and observed. The influence of salt is more subtle. It spreads unseen. It does not reveal itself to the eye. It makes its presence known by mingling unseen in other substances. Its glory is that we rather note its absence than observe its presence. Its function is, without obtruding itself, to make food pleasant and palatable. It thus becomes the fitting emblem of that unconscious influence which is rather of character than of opinion. As light represents the distinct, vigorous, and conscious influence of the intellect, and of the will in active agency: so salt represents that quiet, unspoken, felt, but unobserved influence which disposition or character can exercise.

The influence which a man exercises by the silent force of character and example is often more powerful than that which he wields by conscious and voluntary effort. He exerts his conscious influence when he seeks by argument and persuasion to change men's opinions or to control their actions; but this direct form of attack is not always successful. It may be resented, and even when it seems most successful, it only wins the sullen victory of reluctant assent. But what is not yielded to argument may be surrended to the unspoken power of example. The father in the house may have no sort of power over the growing opinions of his sons and daughters. They listen with superficial deference to his demonstrations, and with scarce concealed amusement to his arguments. Disappointed to find that he fails to carry them with him, he might sadly conclude that his influence in the home was reduced to a cypher. But he would be wrong. The fresh minds of the young generation cannot accept his views: the view-point of the world has changed; the intellectual vantage-ground is no longer the same. But harmony of opinions is not the same as sympathy of spirit; and reverence, affection, devotion, still remain and, in the hands of a true-hearted, upright, loving man, are weightier than arguments in the lips of petulant wisdom.

It is character which gives force to wisdom. Ability without character has often failed to win its way. Peisistratus, we read, was courteous, liberal, affable, his tongue full of kindly inquiries after the sick and unfortunate, his language soft and modest, his gardens thrown open to the public; but there was one fatal flaw. Solon told him that if his virtue had been genuine, he would have been the best citizen in Athens. The coin shone well and was of correct weight, but it lacked the true ring. The light was there, but the salt was wanting. The conscious influence was correct; the unconscious influence betrayed its own unreality. The same thought was expressed somewhat differently by an eminent English judge, who said: "A man's reputation in England depends on his knowledge, his eloquence, and his character." He recognised that light without salt might meet with admiration, but could not secure respect. It is true; for we look that men should be good as well as great. Thought and energy are not sufficient to inspire our confidence. It is the moral force behind these which awakens our trust. When a noble and spiritual character speaks noble thoughts in noble words the people listen; their hearts and consciences respond. Such a man can rebuke wickedness with some hope of provoking shame. Mere ability, speaking on moral questions, can awaken at best a tame acquiescence; it may stir only an unwholesome mirth.

Now these two forces, the conscious and unconscious, the conscious exercise of all our powers for good supported by the unconscious influence of sincere and devoted character, Christ claims for all. These two sorts of influence every man may use. By the one he can be light : by the other he can be salt in the earth.

"Ye are the salt of the earth : ye are the light of the world." The healing influence of character and the illuminating power of truth are both in the hands of men. Both are needful to give the highest and widest range to human influence, and both act and react upon one another. Our thoughts influence our characters; and our characters sway our thoughts. As we think we are, is one side of the truth ; as we are we think, is another. "Stipend," said the frank-spoken Scotch minister, " has a verra strong influence on metapheesics." Noble thoughts, read, received, lived up to, are a perpetual appeal to the moral nature, and help in its formation. It is important to think truly : it is important to be true.

But the danger which besets character is more subtle than the danger which besets opinion. The unconscious influence of life is perhaps more readily injured than its conscious influence. The moral powers are even more delicate, more susceptible of damage and deterioration than are the intellectual. We can hardly degenerate in physical power without being aware of it. We can hardly degenerate in intellectual force without meeting with some failure to remind us of it. But we may degenerate in moral force, and not know it. Like Samson, we may rest in the lap of pleasure while our moral vigour is being slowly impaired. We may sleep and wake, and we may think to go about our work as at other times, and not be aware of the terrible change which has fallen upon us. But power, the most priceless power of all, moral power, the very sceptre of our being, has slipped from our grasp. The sentence of doom is often written against a man, though he knows it not. "He wist not," so it is written of Samson, "that the Lord was departed from him" (Judges xvi. 20). It is this enfeeblement, which creeps upon a man before he is aware of it, which our Lord touches on here. Salt is good, "but if the salt have lost his savour, wherewith shall it be salted?" (Matt. v. 13.) The evaporation has taken place. The virtue has gone out of the mass. In appearance it is just what it was before. In fact it is very different. It is no longer the healing, preserving, beneficent product. It is a whited mass of uselessness. It is fit for nothing. The change has come, but the change has left the appearance unchanged. The change is not noticeable. This is the awful part of the process. A change in opinions is known and recognised; the man himself is aware when he has altered his views. But his character may alter, and he may dream that he is the same man which he was before. But as a fact the strongest and sweetest part of his influence has departed. He may be just as liberal in his donations, he may be just as often to the front in works of beneficence, he may be as frequently on philanthropic and religious platforms, but the whole moral tone of the man is altered. The sacrifice may be seen in the life, but the sacrifice is without the salt. The speech may be as ardently pious as before, but the speech is no longer seasoned with the salt of personal piety. It has become goody instead of good. It is offensive, for it lacks the genuineness which personal devoutness alone can give.

These two, salt and light—what forces they are in human life! Every man who can speak and act among his fellow-men may be a centre of light. Every man who comes into contact with his fellow-men brings to them a clean or an unclean influence. There is the influence of word and deed, which we hear and know, accept or reject; but there is also the subtle, ethical contagion, which may leave us the better or the worse almost without our knowledge. The unwholesome influence of the impure character,

> Like a new disease, unknown to men,
> Creeps—no precautions used—among the crowd.

Who would not fear lest, though no words were spoken, his very presence carried a sort of moral "death among men"? Who would not wish that his influence might always be fresh, pure, health-giving, like salt adding new flavour and force to all that was good? We can understand the apostle's caution: "Take heed unto thyself and unto the doctrine" (1 Tim. iv. 16). Take heed what your known and active influence may be. Take heed to yourself that your unconscious influence may be clean and good also. Conduct is more than creed, and character is more than conduct. Conduct commends our creed, and character gives force to conduct.

And seeing that all our fresh springs are in God, must it not be that in nearness to Him will be found the secret strength of character? Wherewith shall it be salted when once the saltness has departed? We may sadly ask the question, with perhaps the consciousness that we have deteriorated in moral force. Are our lives doomed to uselessness? The salt which can no longer give flavour to the bread in the house is fit neither for the land nor for the dung-hill. No human hand can restore its saltness. The freshness and vigour of simple and genuine character cannot be given back after worldliness, self-indulgence, greed, and pleasure-loving cruelty have done their work, and after the fresh aspirations, emotions, and longings after good, have gone away like the early dew. For love—generous, pure, unselfish love—is the salt of human character; and when the love has passed away the very basis of character has disappeared. No earthly power can restore sweet lovingness to the dead, world-killed heart. But the things which are impossible with man are possible with God. And God, who "commanded the light to shine out of darkness" (2 Cor. iv. 6), can give the hope which maketh not ashamed and "shed abroad the love of God in our hearts by the Holy Ghost which is given unto us" (Rom. v. 5).

THE INNER IS THE HIGHER

Think not that I am come to destroy the law, or the prophets: I am not come to destroy, but to fulfil.

For verily I say unto you, Till heaven and earth pass, one jot or one tittle shall in no wise pass from the law, till all be fulfilled.

Whosoever therefore shall break one of these least commandments, and shall teach men so, he shall be called the least in the kingdom of heaven: but whosoever shall do and teach them, the same shall be called great in the kingdom of heaven.

For I say unto you, That except your righteousness shall exceed the righteousness of the scribes and Pharisees, ye shall in no case enter into the kingdom of heaven.

Ye have heard that it was said by them of old time, Thou shalt not kill; and whosoever shall kill shall be in danger of the judgment.

But I say unto you, That whosoever is angry with his brother without a cause shall be in danger of the judgment: and whosoever shall say to his brother, Raca, shall be in danger of the council; but whosoever shall say, Thou fool, shall be in danger of hell fire.

Therefore if thou bring thy gift to the altar, and there rememberest that thy brother have ought against thee;

Leave there thy gift before the altar, and go thy way; first be reconciled to thy brother, and then come and offer thy gift. . . . .

Ye have heard that it was said by them of old time, Thou shalt not commit adultery:

But I say unto you, That whosoever looketh on a woman to lust after her, hath committed adultery with her already in his heart.

And if thy right eye offend thee, pluck it out, and cast it from thee: for it is profitable for thee that one of thy members should perish, and not that thy whole body should be cast into hell. . . . .

It hath been said, Whosoever shall put away his wife, let him give her a writing of divorcement:

But I say unto you, That whosoever shall put away his wife, saving for the cause of fornication, causeth her to commit adultery: and whosoever shall marry her that is divorced committeth adultery.

Again, ye have heard that it hath been said by them of old time, Thou shalt not forswear thyself, but shalt perform unto the Lord thine oaths:

But I say unto you, Swear not at all. . . . .

But let your communication be, Yea, yea; Nay, nay: for whatsoever is more than these cometh of evil.

Ye have heard that it hath been said, An eye for an eye, and a tooth for a tooth:

But I say unto you, That ye resist not evil: but whosoever shall smite thee on thy right cheek, turn to him the other also. . . . .

Ye have heard that it hath been said, Thou shalt love thy neighbour, and hate thine enemy.

But I say unto you, Love your enemies, bless them that curse you, do good to them that hate you, and pray for them which despitefully use you, and persecute you. . . . .

For if ye love them which love you, what reward have ye? do not even the publicans the same?

And if ye salute your brethren only, what do ye more than others? do not even the publicans so?

Be ye therefore perfect, even as your Father which is in heaven is perfect.

THE INNER IS THE HIGHER

THE section of the Sermon on the Mount, which lies between the seventeenth verse and the closing verse of St. Matthew v., deals with one subject—Christ's relation to the Moral Law.

Christ taught a higher righteousness. His contemporaries were content with the letter of the law. He insisted on its spirit. They thought that an external conformity was sufficient; and the result of this idea was a spirit of legal quibbling and adroit evasion of principles. Men attained the art of measuring acts and ceremonial observances with a faultless nicety; while the heart and soul were left untouched by piety. They sought what was outward. Christ demanded what was within.

It must be remembered that this principle is double edged. It seeks the inward significance of the law, as well as inward loyalty of the heart. The question has been asked whether Jesus Christ did not, notwithstanding His protest that He came not to destroy but to fulfil, weaken the sense of obligation towards the law? Did He not emphasise certain important moral commandments and leave other, perhaps lesser, precepts in the shadow of doubt? If He upheld some great and essential principles of the law, did He not disparage the jot and the tittle of it after all?

It seems clear from the opening words of this section that His attitude towards the law had already been misunderstood or misinterpreted. His teaching had been a free and a joyous teaching of a kingdom which was at hand. There were, doubtless, some who read in His words some latent hostility to existing institutions or laws. And they were right if they read in Christ's words a dissatisfaction with the tone of religious life of His day. But they were wrong if they imagined that He sought to destroy the moral and spiritual code of the law. Such a suspicion Christ seeks to dispel. " Think not that I am come to destroy the law or the prophets," He says, including the prophets in His message, and going beyond some of the contemporary Jews, who made the prophets of less account than the law.

There is a double explicitness about our Lord's teaching. He did not come to destroy the law or the prophets; for in the nature of the case these are indestructible—" Till heaven and earth pass away, one jot or one tittle shall in no wise pass away from the law, till all things be accomplished " (Matt. v. 18, Revised Version). But further, so far from weakening or destroying the law, He had come to give it ampler and fuller meaning—" For I say unto you, That except your righteousness shall exceed the righteousness of the Scribes and Pharisees, ye shall in no case enter into the kingdom of heaven " (Matt. v. 20). He disclaims any attempt to destroy the indestructible. He affirms the necessity of finding in it a larger and richer significance.

1. The moral law is indestructible. It is of the great moral and spiritual teaching of the law and the prophets which our Lord is speaking. He has not at the moment the ceremonial law or the predictions of prophets in mind. It is of righteousness, the great ethical code of existence, that He treats. This will be clear, if we read the whole section, following its simple and obvious suggestions. It is a deep spiritual righteousness which He seeks to enforce. It must be a righteousness greater than that of Scribes and Pharisees. It deals not with mint, anise and cummin, but with weightier matters of the law. It must be a righteousness which touches the mainsprings of the affections and emotions. The examples which our Lord brings

forward are all related to the ethical life. The laws of murder and adultery are treated of. In dealing with these, He comments on commandments in the Decalogue; while He alludes to precepts other than those of the Decalogue, when He speaks of oaths (Ex. xx. 7), of retribution (Lev. xxiv. 20), and of neighbourly love (Lev. xix. 18). But all His allusions are to matters ethical, and not ceremonial. This is the law which is indestructible. The ceremonial law dealt with types and shadows and decaying things which were ready to vanish away (Heb. viii. 13). Coleridge said, "The outward service of ancient religion, the rites, ceremonies and ceremonial vestments of the old law, had morality for their substance. They were the letter of which morality was the spirit; the enigma of which morality was the meaning. But morality itself is the service and ceremonial of the Christian religion." "Pure religion," writes St. James, using a word which expresses the outward show of worship, a pure culture, "and undefiled before God and the Father is this, To visit the fatherless and widows in their affliction, and to keep himself unspotted from the world" (James i. 27). The apostle claims for the new Dispensation, as Archbishop Trench said, a superiority over the old in that its very $\theta\rho\eta\sigma\kappa\epsilon\iota\alpha$ (religion—culture) consists in acts of mercy, of love and of holiness, in that it has light for its garment, its very robe being righteousness. Thus the outward form of religion may perish, but its inward man is renewed. The ethical quality abides when the ceremonial aspect alters.

The law in its noble, ethical sense, Christ did not come to destroy. This law was written on stone, on the imperishable red granite—the symbol of their enduring character. There is no change in the moral law. The basis of moral life remains the same from age to age. While science extends her borders and wins new conquests from the cloud-covered realms of the universe, there are no new discoveries in morality. The duties of man to man and of man to God remain. No changes of time, no enlargement of knowledge, can weaken their obligation. But though time cannot alter the moral laws, subtle distinction, fierce partisanship, greedy self-interest, may blind men to their application. Too often the complete application of these laws has, in the interest of a cause or the supposed interests of religion, been set aside. The old heathen held his right arm aloft out of the baptismal water, refusing to consecrate to holier uses the arm which had struck down his foes, and which should do so again. He at least declined to pretend to accept Christ's complete sovereignty over him. But many baptised Christians keep up the show of faith in Christ, and yet break the law which Christ consecrated by His sanction. We cannot too often or too loudly proclaim, in the ears of Christian Churches and Christian men, these words of our Lord—"I came not to destroy the law."

II. So far from destroying the law, or weakening its force or annulling any of its moral principles, Christ came to give it deeper and fuller meaning. He infused into it fresh vitality by spiritualising its application and so enlarging its scope. The remainder of the chapter (Matt. v.), from the twenty-first verse to the end, contains illustrations of this enlargement and deepening of the force of the law. The least commandment, or what men deemed the least important commandment, was still a divine commandment. To break it, or to teach principles which tend to break it or ignore it, was to forfeit place in the kingdom. The perception of the principles of the kingdom was the justification for the kingdom. To ignore the principles was to show that the loyal spirit was some way lacking. The child-spirit reverenced the Father's will, and the least thing which implied lack of such reverence would be hostile to the son-like spirit. The Pharisees measured obedience by the how much and how little; they weighed obedience and disobedience as though they were quantities measurable by the scales of some curious inquisitor. They did not see that the son-like spirit was essential to the higher righteousness, and that no obedience of an external kind could compensate for the lack of that spirit. Such base and formal obedience as meant a bold eye and a proud glance, or the thought, " I am better than thou," was no true obedience of the laws of the divine kingdom. That kingdom asked the obedience of a loyal, loving, filial heart—an obedience far removed from the Pharisaic range of thought—" I say unto you that, except your righteousness exceed the righteousness of the Scribes and Pharisees, ye shall in no case enter into the kingdom of heaven." If we ask wherein the righteousness of the kingdom exceeded that of the Scribes we shall find the answer in the illustrations and examples which follow. Christ takes the commandments respecting murder, adultery, swearing, retribution, neighbourly duty, and in each case shows their higher and truer meaning in contrast with the traditional glosses and interpretations.

(i.) The law of murder.

" Ye have heard that it was said to [not *by*, as in the Authorised Version] them of old time, Thou shalt not kill; and whosoever shall kill shall be in danger of the judgment." Such is our Lord's account of the law as understood by His hearers. He is clearly putting in brief form the current view of the law of murder. We need hardly ask who are they whom Christ describes as "them of old time." The law, "Thou shalt not kill," was given in the early days of the Israelitish history. The commandment must have been familiar to all Jews. The establishment of the synagogues, after the return from Babylon, gave the opportunity of instruction to the people in every district. There the fundamental law, "Thou shalt not kill," would be taught, but, in addition, the penalty which awaited the breach of the law would be explained. To their ancestors both the law and the penalty had been explained. "Whosoever shall kill shall be in danger of the judgment." Dean Plumptre reminded his readers that in A.D. 1611 the words "shall be in danger of" possessed a more distinctly technical sense than they convey now. They meant, "shall be legally liable to." There were judges and officers of justice in all towns, and to these was entrusted the general administration of justice. Judgment was given by these courts. "Judges and officers shalt thou make thee in all thy gates, which the Lord thy God giveth thee, throughout thy tribes; and they shall judge the people with just judgment" (Deut. xvi. 18).

But Christ introduces a higher view. In noble contrast to what was said to them of old, our Lord unfolds the deeper and more spiritual view. "But I say unto you"—we cannot overlook the calm confidence with which He speaks. The comments and applications of earlier teachers are brushed aside. The teachers of old time taught this limited and insufficient view. They supported themselves by references and authorities; they sought legal and verbal justifications of their opinions; they loved to amass materials in support of their view. But with one word Christ reduces all this laborious method to nothing. He speaks; He relies on no authority; He seeks no rabbinical justification; He is not afraid to expound the law in a large and clear sense; He reaches down to foundation thoughts; He speaks as having unquestioned truth to declare; He doubts not that the consciences of those who hear will respond to the truth when once it is unfolded. "I say unto you that every one who is angry with his brother"—the words "without cause" are wanting in some of the best MSS.—"shall be in danger of the judgment; and whosoever shall say to his brother, Raca, shall be in danger of the council; and whosoever shall say, Thou fool, shall be in danger of the Gehenna of fire." The hearers are directed to look inward. Any one who saw the poor, helpless, silent corpse could condemn the hand which had smitten it down. For any one can be wise after the event. It is proverbial unwisdom which is only wise enough to take precautions after a loss has been sustained. A truer wisdom seeks the sources of calamity. It is a nobler thing, though a less conspicuous service, to prevent a calamity than to remedy it. To the cradle of wrongdoing, accordingly, our Lord leads His hearers. He asks them to notice the heart. Out of it sprang the worst evils of life (Matt. xv. 19). He indicates how from small, but unchecked emotions, evil words and actions spring. There is first the emotion of anger; there is next the heedless word of contempt; there is then the deliberate utterance of more fixed dislike or hatred. The irritated feeling breaks into words; the feeling, cherished and given expression to, passes at length into a more established hostile animus; for a man in momentary irritation may say "Raca"—empty-head, idiot—using the first contemptuous word which is at hand; but he exhibits a sort of malignant judgment when he declares his brother to be a wicked and godless fool. This is the distinction which according to Lightfoot lies between the two words—Raca and fool. The first, Raca, he explains as a Jewish nickname; it is so used in the Talmud; it is a despiteful title to a despised man.

So Lightfoot, who gives a story in illustration: "Our Rabbis show a thing done with a religious man, that was praying in the highway: by comes a great man, and gives him the time of the day: but he saluted him not again: he stayed for him, till he had finished his prayer: after he had done his prayer, he said to him, 'Reka, is it not written in your law, that you shall take heed to yourselves? Had I struck off thy head with my sword, who should have required thy blood?' And so goes the angry man on." Lightfoot further quotes a phrase of Irenæus, which in his view comes near to Raca, "Qui exspuit cerebrum, a man that hath no brains." So Raca signifies a man empty, whether of understanding or goodness (Lightfoot, "Erubhim or Miscellanies," Works, vol. iv. pp. 27, 28). "Raca" denotes indeed morosity, and lightness of manners and life; but "fool" judges bitterly of the spiritual and eternal state, and decreeth a man to certain destruction (Lightfoot, Works, vol. xi. p. 109). It is one thing to condemn the intellectual weakness of a brother: it is another to sit in judgment on his moral state. In the one case we may be, and probably are, wrong; in the other case, we are striving to climb into heaven on the supposition that our brother is worthy of hell. But worse, we are hardening our hearts against our brother. We have allowed feelings to find expression in hasty words, and we have allowed a settled dislike to utter itself in words of harsh condemnation. In doing so we have barred our hearts with iron bars against our brother, and we have lost the power of doing him justice. All who know the development and operations of the heart know how quickly we may pass from momentary irritation to passionate language, and from passionate language into a fixed attitude of unjust hatred. Such is the climax of the heart's emotions which Christ sketches. He stops short of the dark final scene, in which the apt hand has done the fatal injury. But we all know that behind the curtain that last scene may be enacted. Our Lord does not say that the angry thought is as bad as the murderous deed, but He does say that the angry thought may be the first stage of a downward career: He does say that disturbed emotions, angry and resentful feelings, are not innocent, and may be dangerous. He carries the law back into the arena of the dispositions. To be good, it is needful that the heart be good.

To be godlike it is needful not only that the actions should be blameless but that the thoughts of the heart should be noble, calm and generous. Evil dispositions, wrathful sentiments arising from irritated feelings, bring a man within range of condemnation—in danger of judgment, of council, of the Gehenna of fire. In these words, judgment, council, Gehenna are clear allusions to Jewish customs and scenes. The judgment takes us to the local court: the council to the great court of the Sanhedrim: the Gehenna of fire to the valley of Hinnom. There is a climax in the condemnation as there had been in the offences. Lesser offences and lesser punishments were in the hands of a lower tribunal consisting of seven men. Serious offences and severe penalties belonged to the Sanhedrim. Seventy, or more, members, the twenty-four heads of the priestly courses, together with forty-six (or forty-eight) elders or scribes, constituted this higher national court. Offences such as blasphemy came within their cognizance; and they alone had the power of ordering death by stoning, and from their sentence there was no appeal. By their order Stephen suffered; and of our Lord they cried, "He hath spoken blasphemy." Gehenna is the Greek form of Gehinnom, the Valley of Hinnom, the narrow gorge on the south of Jerusalem, always associated with burnings or fires which were kindled there. There in degenerate days children had been made to pass through the fire of Moloch (1 Kings xi. 7; 2 Kings xvi. 3; 2 Chron. xxviii. 3; xxxiii. 6). Josiah defiled it (2 Kings xxiii. 10-14), and in later times it was the spot where the refuse of the city was destroyed. The place where the false and cruel gods had been worshipped became the place where useless and unclean things were destroyed. Here was the consuming fire which burned continually. It became the image of the lot of the reprobate. It was the common sink of the whole city; whither all filthiness and all kind of nastiness met. . . . . And there was there also a continual fire, whereby bones and other filthy things were consumed, lest they might offend or infect the city (Lightfoot, Works, vol. x. p. 81). Christ teaches that where the fire of wrath burns fiercely in a man's bosom, the man is in danger of meeting fire. Those who heat the flame ten times hotter are in danger of being themselves consumed. Norfolk counsels Buckingham,

> " Be advised,
> Heat not a furnace for your foe so hot
> That it do singe yourself."
>
> *King Henry VIII.* act i. sc. 1.

But Norfolk was only warning of the injury which a much provoked enemy might inflict. There is a worse injury and a more fearsome burning which heated wrath may bring, the fire which he brings on himself. The inward moral wrong which persistent evil habits occasion is as the beginning of hell. This is the burden which a man's own misdeeds lay upon him and yet not his misdeeds only, but also indulged evil dispositions. "In that mysterious condition of the depraved will, compelled, yet free, the slave of sinful habit, yet responsible for every act of sin, and gathering deeper condemnation as the power of amendment grows less and less, may we not see," asked Dean Mansel, " some possible foreshadowing of the yet deeper guilt and the yet more hopeless misery of the worm that dieth not and the fire that is not quenched?" (Bampton Lectures, pp. 157, 8).

Having thus vividly pictured the stages of growing wrath and the darker doom to which it must lead, our Lord urges the habit of never allowing the ill-feeling time to grow into an overmastering passion. The hour of worship, which He assumes to be natural to His hearers, brings the opportunity of self-vigilance. The man is about to approach God in worship. As he does so, let him take account of himself. Those who bear the vessels of the sanctuary should be clean; and no evil which can be removed should be suffered to linger in the heart of him who draws near to God. How can a man with son-like confidence approach his Father in heaven, while his bosom swells with unseemly wrath or is the arena of unbrotherly feelings?

Yes, if even in the sanctuary itself the sense of discord, misunderstanding, and soreness remain,

pause, postpone your worship; seek reconciliation with your brother before you make your offering—
" If therefore thou art offering thy gift at the altar, and there rememberest that thy brother hath aught against thee, leave there thy gift before the altar, and go thy way, first be reconciled to thy brother, and then come and offer thy gift." First the brother, then the Father. Every son of God comes into His presence as one of a brotherhood. And at all worship God seems to ask of each worshipper, How is it with thy brother? The thought of the sacrifice of Cain rises in our mind. In it the illustration of the wrathful spirit gains force from the remembrance of the deed of blood which followed. God receives no sacrifice from the soul which is swelling with wrath. The very purpose of worship is lost sight of, when no self-questioning goes with it. The value of the religious ordinance is destroyed; the sacrifice is profaned. The spirit of self-deception is evoked when we persist in imagining that we can draw near to God, when we in spirit are far from love, and are casting His words behind us. We are giving then what is holy to the dogs: the beast of anger will tread the spirit of worship under foot. It is vain to stay in the sanctuary. We must face the wild beast and slay it. We must go and be reconciled to our brother, and then, but not till then, offer

our gift. How much is the profit of worship spoiled by the neglect of this counsel of Christ? How many on the Sunday, as they go to church, ask if a brother has aught against them? God, we say, must come first; His worship must not be neglected. True, but reconciliation is worship, and so Christ says, "First, *first* be reconciled to thy brother."

Where the teaching here enunciated is not understood, the most elementary principle of true religion has yet to be learned. To imagine that sacrifice is everything, or, indeed, anything apart from the moral condition of him who offers it, is to degrade religion into ceremonial, and to rob the idea of righteousness from our notion of God. Yet this was precisely what the Jews were prone to do. An error in ceremonial was more than a defect in moral disposition. It was the same with the religion of Latium, where sacrificial exactitude was everything and the heart of the worshipper nothing. But Christ demands that there shall be harmony between the soul and the act of worship: the one shall be the true outcome of the other. The Jews provided that a sacrifice might be postponed where the offerer owed pecuniary damages to his brother man; but Christ enlarges the obligation. "If thy brother hath *aught* against thee!"

Our Lord further enforces the thought by an

illustration which takes us back to the tribunal of justice. He would have us remember the strict justice which governs all. While we are on earth we have the opportunity of living in loving and brotherly fashion with our neighbours. If we have wronged them, the chance as well as the duty of reconciliation is ours. If we have acted so that we have changed a neighbour into an enemy, it is our wisdom and our duty to seek to make him a friend again. Our life should not be strewn with stones which we have cast in our brother's way. Still less should we imagine that the placing of such stumbling-blocks before his feet is no matter. If of every idle word men shall give account, how much more must we expect to be called to account for those angry, mischievous words or malicious acts which have made life harder to our brother men? "Agree with thine adversary quickly, whiles thou art with him in the way; lest haply the adversary deliver thee to the judge, and the judge deliver thee to the officer, and thou be cast into prison. Verily I say unto thee, Thou shalt by no means come out thence, till thou have paid the uttermost farthing." There is no heaven without heavenly dispositions. He who harbours unbrotherly feelings, keeps up quarrels, ignores the injuries which he may have done to his neighbours, and lives therefore in indifference to the law of love which is the law of the divine kingdom binding man to man, is outside the kingdom, and must remain for ever outside; for the hell of his own heart makes every place hell. If we set beside this picture of the adversary and the judge that other picture which Christ gave of the doom of those who left their brethren in hunger, in sickness, and in prison, we get the two sides of the duty of love—one the duty of reconciliation, the other the duty of practical kindness. In both cases the doom comes not because of actual sin, but because of omitted duty; while in one case it is clear that the true meaning of life is not understood, in the other the true spirit of love is not at work. Love should animate the heart. We should live by it. This love should be free, frank, generous and kindly. Indifference to a brother's needs or injuries should be impossible. Hence in our Lord's view the law of love is violated when from lack of brotherly disposition a man wittingly leaves his neighbour to perish; and the sixth commandment is broken whenever we harbour those angry or malevolent feelings which blind us to the bond of brotherhood with which a fatherly love has bound man to man.

(ii.) The law of adultery.

Once we have grasped the principle which our Lord employs, the application becomes easy. The

principle is simple. It lies in the word love. This carries us into the region of the spirit; it reminds us that the act has its significance from the spirit. The act is the outward and visible sign of what has been going on in the heart. Where love is true and pure, there loyalty, honour, a deep and reverent regard for the brotherhood will be found. The soul will be sensitive to a disloyal thought, just as it will repress the angry feeling. Love triumphs over wrath, for love is kind. Love also triumphs over lust, for it purges affection of its earthliness. Where the dispositions of the soul are pure and right, there the selfish, greedy look will not be seen. Where desire is sundered from the true love which seeks the good of its object, there is sin. Christ speaks indeed of one form of sin, but the principle is true of many others. Whenever men are regarded and used as the means of gratifying some greedy and selfish desire, whenever selfishness makes us forget the good of those whom we employ for our comfort and ease, there sin is not lacking: desire is sundered from love. Pure love would rather endure any pain or privation than make men the victims of selfishness. Therefore it follows—
" If thy right eye causeth thee to stumble, pluck it out, and cast it from thee; for it is profitable for thee that one of thy members should perish, and

not thy whole body be cast into Gehenna. And if thy right hand causeth thee to stumble, cut it off, and cast it from thee; for it is profitable for thee that one of thy members should perish, and not thy whole body go into Gehenna." The words, it is needless to say, are not to be taken literally; the plucking out of the physical eye would not cure the wandering desire; the cutting off of the right hand would not banish selfish dispositions. Some, indeed, have taken the words literally, and have acted as though bodily dismemberment was equivalent to spiritual safety. What is meant is that all the powers of body, soul, and life may be made instruments of wrong; and that it is better therefore to forego whatever is innocent in itself if it becomes a cause of evil to us.

Here we touch a great principle which, perhaps, more than any other the religious world has found it difficult to understand. The principle is that if any man finds certain things, innocent in themselves, the cause of spiritual injury to him, he had better abandon them. This involves the thought that one man may find injury where another finds none. The right eye may cause offence to one; the right hand may be the cause to another. The sacrifice in the one case is not the same as in the other: each man must sacrifice that which proves to be a snare to himself. Music, art, the drama, meat and drink are in themselves innocent; but all may become snares to men, though not all to every man. In so far as we find them becoming ministers of harm to us, let us be ready to sacrifice taste and inclination to preserve moral vigour and purity; but let us not insist that the sacrifice which is needful for us is essential to the religious life of others. And yet let all remember that there are few to whom some right hand or right eye may not bring temptation.

Alongside the question of purity of desire, Christ places the question of divorce. The dissolution of the marriage tie among the Jews was practically allowed on the most trivial occasions. As a fact, mere lightness, fickleness, the decay of the old love, or the lighting of new desire led to divorce. Christ has touched upon this wandering desire. The look was sin; yet this passing desire was in Jewish customs allowed a legal opportunity of indulgence. When tired of his wife or attracted by some one else, a man might by a stroke of the pen get rid of the inconvenient wife.

The transition in the verses now becomes clear. The look of lust is sin. But it was said, "Whosoever shall put away his wife, let him give her a writing of divorcement." This came to mean the permission to any man who had a new fancy, to gratify it at the expense of the wife whom he was bound to sustain and cherish. This was sin: it was adultery, though carried on under *quasi* legal sanction. "But I say unto you, that every one that putteth away his wife, saving for the cause of fornication, maketh her an adulteress; and whosoever shall marry her when she is put away committeth adultery." Jewish opinion was divided as to the grounds on which divorce was permissible. The school of Hillel was lax. A man might get rid of his wife if her habits were bad, or if she did not cook to her husband's satisfaction. The passage in Deut. xxiv. 1 was quoted to justify his putting her away if he met any one who was more pleasing in his eyes. The school of Shammai took a stricter and nobler view. A man ought not to put away his wife, except for adultery. Our Lord's view is in harmony with this teaching. The laxity of the other school He condemns. The letter kills; the spirit gives life. And He taught His disciples to look inward, to catch the spirit of the law, and to judge themselves not by conformity to some quibbling interpretation, but by the dispositions and affection of the heart. In listening to Christ, we pass into a higher region: the small, technical and verbal arguments of the Scribes and Pharisees disappear. We feel that the character cannot be measured by the standard of an attorney but by its general moral attitude towards righteousness and love.

(iii.) The law of speech.

Our Lord introduces His teaching on this matter by reference to the existing customs of the Jews, sanctioned by some ancient interpretation—"Ye have heard that it was said to them of old time, Thou shalt not forswear thyself, but shalt perform unto the Lord thine oaths." We trace in this traditional teaching that strange mixture of falseness and religiousness, which is so fatal to genuine religion. Perjury was forbidden, but the question might still be what was perjury, and when was a man forsworn? The precept in Lev. xix. 12, was, "Ye shall not swear by my name falsely, neither shalt thou [so that thou, R.V.] profane the name of thy God: I am the Lord;" But it is clear from our Lord's words that many oaths were permitted by the Jewish practice, the violation of which did not constitute, in their eyes, perjury. Some oaths therefore, if violated, meant perjury: some did not. Light comes to us on this matter from the story of our Lord's trial. When the high priest adjured Him by the living God, he sought to put Him to an oath, the desecration of which would be perjury. But other oaths might be taken. The street and the market-place might ring with vehement asseverations and hard swearing. The dealer might invoke all sorts of attestations in order to persuade the buyer. We can transport ourselves into the Eastern bazaar: we can hear the loud voices bargaining in extravagant language, and the ready oaths to beguile the customer. The moral sense of the inhabitants is not shocked. It is true that the place resounds with hard and false swearing; but there is no harm in it. "Everybody does it: it deceives nobody." We know these old and misleading pleas of falsehood. This was bad enough. But there was worse behind. Men might be loose, false, or criminally careless towards their fellow-men. They might mislead by untrue statements, backed up by the nimble or solemn sounding oath; and yet be guiltless of perjury. But if they had promised some sacrifice, perhaps vowed a vow, should their fraudulent dealing prove successful, they must be scrupulous to fulfil this oath. It was a religious bond: it must be straitly observed; whatever moral laxity was allowed in dealings with men, the Temple sacrifice must be offered. Thus an untrue distinction between moral and religious obligation was set up. It was forgotten, or never realized, that if a man deceives his brother man by urgent oath, his offering is unacceptable to God. On the altar the gift must be left unoffered till the wrong done to the brother has been set right. "If a man love not his brother whom he hath seen, how can he love God whom he hath not seen."

In contradistinction to the immoral religionism of Jewish practice, our Lord sets up the supremacy of those simple moral principles which are essential to religion. In dealing with men, all these specious and by no means innocent oaths were to be set aside. Dealings between man and man should be conducted on principles of simple truthfulness, which needed no extravagant protestation and adroit swearing. Simple affirmation concerning the matter in hand ought to be sufficient. Honesty needs not the support of the loud oath or the invocation of sacred names. Swear not at all, for every oath is in the last resort an appeal to the judgment of heaven. It is not the one solemn adjuration by the name of the living God, which makes the oath an appeal to the divine knowledge: all that is sacred is sacred only through Him who is the sanctifying life of all things. The solemnity of the sanction and the responsibility of the invocation cannot be lessened by swearing by lesser things, by heaven or earth, by Jerusalem, by the head; for the oath by these things carries you into God's presence. Heaven is the throne of God; earth is the footstool of God; Jerusalem is the city of the great King.

The head by which you swear is subject to the laws of God. It is a vain thing to attempt to evade God, whose presence, power, and life are everywhere. You cannot avoid His laws or His kingdom. If you take the wings of the morning, or dream that the darkness can cover you, even there will His hand find you. It is as impossible to find immunity from His scrutiny in the empty subterfuge or the verbal quibble. He must be all or nothing in the life of man. And every action of man should be done as in His presence. In the recognition of that presence, sober speech and simple truthfulness are best. "Let your speech be Yea, yea, Nay, nay; and whatsoever is more than these is of evil (or the evil one, R. V.)" Thus does our Lord bring a deep solemnity into all the simplest words and acts of life. He is religious who is filled with a religious sense so deep and strong that it permeates all his deeds and all his speech. Such a one will make no distinction between the obligation of the word spoken in the market and the word spoken in the temple. Utter truthfulness must be in both. Still less can such a man excuse the fraud of the street by the sacrifice on the altar. May such a one take an oath? Does our Lord forbid the solemn oath for purposes of justice or evidence? If we pay heed to the intention and aim of our Lord's teaching, we shall find nothing which forbids such oaths. What he aimed at was the inveterate and deceitful habit of using oaths and protestations to throw a brother man off his guard, and to win some advantage from him. Nevertheless our Lord's teaching sets before us an ideal community in which such entire truthfulness prevailed that no solemn adjuration would be needful, for a man's word would be as good as his oath or his bond.

(IV.) The law of retribution.

The law of retribution as accepted among the Jews was the simple one—"An eye for an eye, and a tooth for a tooth." The penalty and the offence were to be the same. It was the law of the strictest *quid pro quo*. The particulars are set forth with more fulness in Exodus xxi. 24. There is a sense in which a very just and careful law of retribution is probably necessary in a community. Lynch law, which is a kind of wild justice, is possibly indispensable in an unformed society. It is the ready means of bringing untamed and unscrupulous spirits into order and discipline. But there is a great difference between the law of the State which is protective and above all littleness and spite, and the law which should regulate personal dealings between man and man. The Jews had made the general law of retribution as stated in

Exodus xxi. a kind of principle of personal conduct instead of a code of instruction to be used by judges. In all societies there must be a difference between the mode of dealing between individual and individual, and between authorities and individuals. The law of kindness, the sentiment of benevolence, has naturally a freer and more legitimate scope in individual life than in public life; there are actions which would be right and laudable in a man, which would be unjustifiable in a judge. On the other hand, he is a poor citizen who makes the strictness of the law the measure of his private actions. This is Shylock and his pound of flesh.

Now, against this perversion of matters, Christ enters His protest. The spirit which should animate the private citizen should be the spirit of kindness, patience, ready helpfulness. He should be disposed to put up with inconveniences, and even injustice. The spirit of retaliation is alien to the Son of God. The only retaliation which He inculcates is that retaliation which overcomes evil with good—" I say unto you, Resist not him that is evil; but whosoever smiteth thee on thy right cheek, turn to him the other also. And if any man would go to law with thee, and take away thy coat, let him have thy cloke also. And whosoever shall compel thee to go one mile, go with him twain.

Give to him that asketh thee, and from him that would borrow of thee turn not thou away." There can be no doubt that our Lord here inculcated a habit of life which shows a strong belief in the power of good. He teaches us after a fashion which implies that in the long run good is stronger than evil, kindness than cruelty, love than law. This is the spirit of His teaching. This was the spirit of His action also. Do not rely on law or on force to obtain what you desire. Rely rather on those greater laws and forces of righteousness and love which rule the universe. Be patient under injury. Be cheerful under inconvenience.

It is perhaps needless to say that our Lord does not even imply the unlawfulness of the vocation of the magistrate or the policeman. He is speaking throughout of personal action under personal injury. There is no hint that He condemns those who exert their power to the utmost to protect the weak and the oppressed. Men may very lawfully do on behalf of others that which they would not do for themselves. Civil magistracy, properly administered, is a protective force. The degree in which we should invoke its protection is left to ourselves. The counsel of Christ is to rely rather on moral force than on legal power; but in counselling this, He by no means censures the existence of tribunal or judge.

(v.) The law of neighbourliness.

Here again the Jews had given a harsh turn to the law of Moses.—" Ye have heard that it was said, Thou shalt love thy neighbour, and hate thine enemy." This ancient saying was a simple perversion of Old Testament precepts. In Levit. xix. 17, 18, we find this precept—"Thou shalt not hate thy brother in thine heart. . . . Thou shalt not take vengeance, nor bear any grudge against the children of thy people, but thou shalt love thy neighbour as thyself." The inference which the fierce nationalism of the Jews derived from these precepts was that it was lawful to hate those who were not their brethren. The stranger and the foreigner was a legitimate object of hatred. It is easy to see how this perversion might receive an extended meaning. The private enemy is regarded as dangerous: personal affronts are exaggerated into offences against society: the unfortunate offender becomes the foe of the nation, for a false citizen is worse than an open foe. But this was not the intentional or original meaning of the precept, Thou shalt hate thine enemy. It meant, Thou shalt hate the foe of Israel. Thus the current Jewish teaching produced narrowness and prejudice. Large-heartedness became impossible. Against it our Lord sets the noble ideal, which even yet is beyond the power of the world to reach.—"I say unto you, Love your enemies, and pray for them that persecute you; that ye may be sons of your Father which is in heaven; for He maketh His sun to rise on the evil and the good. . . . . For if ye love them that love you, what reward have ye? do not even the publicans the same? And if ye salute your brethren only, what do ye more than others? do not even the Gentiles the same?" Here we reach the true elevation of spirit which should mark the child of God. He is in the world for a specific purpose—to do good and to be good. His influence and his energy are precious gifts to be used for the good of man. It is not for him to restrain his hand or to limit the range of his influence. Whenever the opportunity of good comes, there he must do the good. It is not for him to choose upon whom he will use his influence. He must seek to do good to all whom the providence of God brings across his path, as Christ showed in the parable of the Good Samaritan. In God's hand and bounty there is no straitness and no regard of the persons of men. His sun and the rain fall upon the evil and the good; so free and rich must the benevolence of His children be. To do good only among those who are fond of us, or of whom we are fond, is just crude nature and shows no growing and no disciplined affection. The most benighted people will show reciprocal kindness. The sons of God, like their Father, must evince the spirit of beneficence even where there is no chance of reciprocity; for they are to be causes of good in others who are not good. Their aim must be to resemble their Father. If they are good like Him, they will do good like Him, with that large-hearted, impartial and open-handed kindness which God shows in His sunshine and His rain. Like Him, our lives must shed light and refreshment, softening and enriching human hearts by the steady outflow of love. If we are God's children, we shall count it the highest happiness to be like Him. And so with a promise which is also a precept Christ closes His teaching about neighbourliness—"Ye therefore shall be perfect, as your heavenly Father is perfect."

MARKETABLE RELIGION

Take heed that ye do not your alms before men, to be seen of them: otherwise ye have no reward of your Father which is in heaven.

Therefore when thou doest thine alms, do not sound a trumpet before thee, as the hypocrites do in the synagogues and in the streets, that they may have glory of men. Verily I say unto you, They have their reward.

But when thou doest alms, let not thy left hand know what thy right hand doeth:

That thine alms may be in secret: and thy Father which seeth in secret himself shall reward thee openly.

And when thou prayest, thou shalt not be as the hypocrites are: for they love to pray standing in the synagogues and in the corners of the streets, that they may be seen of men. Verily I say unto you, They have their reward.

But thou, when thou prayest, enter into thy closet, and when thou hast shut thy door, pray to thy Father which is in secret; and thy Father which seeth in secret shall reward thee openly.

But when ye pray, use not vain repetitions, as the heathen do: for they think that they shall be heard for their much speaking.

Be not ye therefore like unto them: for your Father knoweth what things ye have need of, before ye ask him.

After this manner therefore pray ye: Our Father which art in heaven, Hallowed be thy name.

Thy kingdom come. Thy will be done in earth, as it is in heaven.

Give us this day our daily bread.

And forgive us our debts, as we forgive our debtors.

And lead us not into temptation, but deliver us from evil: For thine is the kingdom, and the power, and the glory, for ever. Amen.

For if ye forgive men their trespasses, your heavenly Father will also forgive you:

But if ye forgive not men their trespasses, neither will your Father forgive your trespasses.

Moreover when ye fast, be not, as the hypocrites, of a sad countenance: for they disfigure their faces, that they may appear unto men to fast. Verily I say unto you, They have their reward.

But thou, when thou fastest, anoint thine head, and wash thy face;

That thou appear not unto men to fast, but unto thy Father which is in secret: and thy Father, which seeth in secret, shall reward thee openly.

MARKETABLE RELIGION

THE publicity of actions is a foe of sincerity. Everything which is publicly done invites either the praise or blame of men. Too often a man is tempted to rest in this human criticism. The approval of men justifies his merit. Their disapproval is his greatest pain. This condition of things sets up fictitious standards of what is good or bad, well or ill done. Simplicity, which is unaffected nature in action, is destroyed. The action is done for applause. Soon another deterioration takes place. The action is done in the way which is most likely to provoke applause. The trick of playing to the gallery is learned. The man ceases to act in the pure and noble sense; in a lower sense, he is acting in all that he does.

Christ points out this snare and cautions against a corresponding loss. The snare is righteousness followed for reputation's sake: the caution He gives is against loss of the Father's reward. We shall best understand the loss which ensues by understanding the effect of the snare.

The snare is not that which arises out of the baser and more obviously wicked passions. One of the trials or disciplines of life is found in the fact that the higher we climb the more subtle are the temptations, because we move so to speak into a more refined atmosphere. The difference between right and wrong is measured by a more sensitive balance, being altogether occupied with more delicate materials. As long as the question of right and wrong is exhibited in the material sphere, the censure and the applause are meted out by an obvious law. The man who violates the decalogue in open, physical fashion can hardly escape his own condemnation. He knows that he stole, lied, was guilty of uncleanness. The thing is obvious. He may make excuses: doubtless he does: but he does so as one who is quite aware that his action was a breach of the moral law. But when we rise higher in the scale of civilisation or religious discipline, and reach that state or condition of life in which obvious breaches of the moral law are outrages on the customs of society, we are exposed to subtler temptations. We are socially well-behaved men. We have not broken the Commandments. Our hands are clean: there is no blood on them. Our behaviour is pure:

we have been faithful in wedded life. Our treasure-house is honest: what lies there is our hard-earned wealth. Where can any one find fault with us? Nay more, our religion is no mere negative thing. We can do more than claim that we have not broken these clear commandments of God. We have been generous supporters of good causes: we have put our hands into our pockets to relieve the poor. We have been liberal according to our means. Who can find fault with us? Can we even find fault with ourselves?

Now this is in a sort the state of society which Christ has in His mind. The lives of the better class of Jews were comparatively and outwardly pure. They reverenced the law of Moses. They might explain away the more severe precepts; they might indulge in some verbal quibbles. But they would not deny the obligation of the Commandments. They prided themselves on their loyalty to them. Their language if not their spirit would have been that of the young ruler: "All these I have kept from my youth up." The society which they represented was one in which gross outward disregard of moral principles was unfashionable. The religious observance of the law was expected. Some would keep it more exactly than others. Beyond the limits of moral obligation the religious duties of piety would be observed. A man's purity would be measured by his external conformity to the moral law: his piety would be measured by the sedulousness and exactness with which he observed his religious duties. Our Lord deals with three of these: Almsgiving, Prayer and Fasting. In this chapter we shall consider the snares of almsgiving and the antidotes suggested by our Lord.

But the first verse of the chapter (Matt. vi.) seems to contain a general caution against the vicious principle which might infect the performance of all these religious duties. In a society in which the fulfilment of religious duties is approved and fashionable, the temptation to ostentation becomes strong. Indeed, it is only too human a weakness to find pleasure in the applause of our good deeds. Self-approval, when sanctioned and endorsed by popular applause, encourages and confirms our self-esteem. It is, moreover, appetising: it makes us long for more. It tempts us to repeat the experiment that we may taste once again what was so pleasant. And thus purity of motive is ensnared. The sweet tender human impulses out of which these acts of piety should naturally take their origin become tainted and defiled. We do our righteousness before men, to be seen of them. There is no benediction for such deeds, because there is no benevolence in them.

Thus the appearance of piety might remain while the emotions of piety were dead. Men act then not from an inward impulse, but from an outward stimulus. They are like the animal which in obedience to an electric battery simulates the movements of life long after it is dead. They have a name to live and are dead. Their reward is the reward of the dead, they can have none from the living God.

1. *Almsgiving and its snares.*

There are three evils which wait on beneficence.

The act of kindness may be accompanied by a gush of emotion which loses sight of the real need of the recipient. In this case it is rather the indulgence of a sentiment than an act of true beneficence. Self-consciousness, the almost invariable companion of sentimentalism, disturbs the judgment and to a degree also the simplicity of the action. The luxury of doing good becomes, in this case, an almost morbid self-indulgence. Manly feeling dwindles to a self-pleasing emotion. Thoughtfulness for the needy which ought to signalise true benevolence has no place in such sentimentalism. This is that hysterical flabbiness which sins through indiscriminate charity and writes itself down as bountiful when it is little more than self-indulgent and probably mischievous. This is an evil which waits on beneficence —the evil of self-conscious sentiment.

There is another evil. It is perhaps a worse one. Beneficence is accompanied by self satisfaction. It true that there is a God-ordained joy which accompanies all doing good. But this, which is in itself a sort of ruined relic of the ideal life and spirit, becomes easily converted into self-satisfaction, and self-satisfaction becomes self-applause, and self-applause is sometimes mistaken for divine approval. We have earned some right, we think, to divine favour. We have done His work in the world. He will consider our merit. We then begin to speculate whether our acts of benevolence, our generosity in almsgiving, may not win by right the favour of the Almighty. Does not the good man obtain some claim upon God? Does not his liberality, which is piety beyond the negative requirements of the decalogue, give him a right to expect some favour or protection or reward which less righteous or less pious men could not claim? This is the evil of legalism.

There is a third evil. Acts of beneficence are not long the property of the benefactor and the benefited. They become public property. Men's deeds are canvassed. Large bounty is contrasted with lesser. Distinction of position and consideration of relative ability are not very delicately weighed. The world judges by broad results. The act which has been most splendid and most obvious strikes the popular imagination. Beneficence, if it is large enough and conspicuous enough, bribes public sentiment and wins its applause. Beneficence becomes practised for the sake of the public esteem it brings. Let us be bountiful. It enhances our reputation. This is the third evil which waits on beneficence. It is beneficence done for ostentation.

It will be seen that these three evils are corruptions of threefold duty. We owe a duty to God, to man, and to ourselves. When we act beneficently from motives of mere sentiment, we act self-pleasingly rather than with true benevolence. We are really thinking of ourselves more than of our neighbour at such a time. When our beneficence is legalistic, we wrong God by the commercial expectations which we cherish as the reward of our good deeds. When ostentation governs our actions, we introduce an influence which ought to have no place in our motives. The good to be done should be done because of simple and thoughtful kindness. We wrong ourselves when we allow the motives of reputation or the applause of men to mar the simplicity of true benevolence. Sentimentalism looks for reward from self. Legalism looks for reward from God. Ostentation looks for reward from men. And this expectation of, or looking for, reward is an intrusion upon the purity of benevolence: the sweet single-mindedness, the entire naturalness of kindness is impaired.

II. With the remembrance of these three corruptions of benevolence, let us turn to our Lord's teaching. Does He supply us with antidotes to these evils?

He supplies the antidote to the last of the three corruptions—ostentation. It is this with which He concludes this portion of His sermon: "Take heed that ye do not (we must not read 'your alms,' but, as in the Revised Version) your righteousness before men, to be seen of them." The great Hebraist Lightfoot argued that though righteousness was the true meaning, yet righteousness in this case stood for alms, since, according to well-known Jewish usage, alms were often spoken of as righteousness. "They called alms by the name of righteousness" ("Hor. Hebraicæ," Works, vol. xi. p. 131). This may be the case, and yet it seems that the first verse of the chapter contains a general caution which is applicable to the three acts of piety of which He afterwards treats—viz., Almsgiving, Prayer, and Fasting. However this may be, He opens with a caution against the evil of ostentation.

The ostentation might take a very offensive form. It might, not only, delight in applause and therefore court publicity, but it might even condescend to self-advertisement. The trumpet might be sounded before it. It is needless perhaps to inquire whether any such custom existed as the literal blowing of a trumpet to announce an act of beneficence. It is enough that our Lord cautions against the self-vaunting, self-displaying sort of charity which is not content unless its good deeds are chronicled. In the present day the caution might have been, "Do not be desirous that your munificence shall be noticed in the daily papers." Benevolence, so far as it is true and simple benevolence, does not need any such recognition, or any such stimulus as this. The Jews perceived this principle, and, to a degree, acted on it. Lightfoot mentions that there was in the Temple the "Treasury of the Silent, whither some very religious men brought their alms in silence and privacy, when the poor children of good men were maintained." He also quotes a saying which strikingly expresses the same principle of action: "He that doth alms in secret is greater than our master Moses himself." One greater than Moses teaches the same. Against all self-display He gives the precept:—"When therefore, thou doest alms, sound not a trumpet before thee, as the hypocrites do in the synagogues and in the streets, that they may have glory of men. Verily I say unto you, They have their reward. But when thou doest alms, let not thy left hand know what thy right hand doeth, that thine alms may be in secret; and thy Father which seeth in secret shall recompense thee" (Matt. vi. 2).

The second snare is legalism. Has our Lord any caution against this? This is not so obvious as in the former case. Yet it is well to remember the prevalent teaching among the Jews. "Alms were called righteousness in that the Fathers of the Traditions taught, and the common people believed, that alms conferred very much to justification" (Lightfoot, *ibid.*).

"For one farthing given to a poor man in alms, a man is made partaker of the beatifical vision;" or again, "This money goes for alms, that my sons may live, and that I may obtain the world to come." There is the touch of a reward approaching the spiritual in these sayings. But there is also a flavour of bargaining in them. This feature shows itself in utterances such as the following: "A man's table now expiates by alms, as heretofore the altar did by sacrifice." It is true that such a sentiment might have originated in the harmless belief that beneficence and mercy were better than burnt-offerings. It would then run parallel to the sacred writer's precept: "To do good and to communicate forget not; for with such sacrifices God is well pleased" (Heb. xiii. 16). But there is a nobler and freer spirit in the scriptural teaching. No thought of personal advantage, whether of protection or profit, such as that which is present in the Jewish utterance, finds place in the sacred writer's words. And as we turn to another Jewish saying we shall find the motive of personal safety set forth almost without reserve: "If you afford alms out of your purse, God will keep you from all damage and harm." In this utterance there is the thought of a bargain with God. It is true that our Lord does not explicitly deal with this vicious aspect of almsgiving; but inasmuch as He wishes His hearers to measure all actions by the thought of Him who is the Father of men, He inculcates a spirit which would soar above any such low or crude idea. A good man could not make such a contract with God. It would alter the foundation of his faith. He could not do it, for a compact of this kind is based upon a sort of distrust; and a Father must before all be trusted. He could not do it, for it would imply that the favour of God was to be purchased; and the heart of a son could not doubt a Father's care. It, moreover, would seem to make his own piety contingent on the expectation of a particular line of God's providence; whereas true piety was the outcome of a filial relationship, and had as its basis a loving confidence and an unquestioning reverence. Thus our Lord implicitly rebukes the legal spirit in acts of piety. He uses language which makes such a spirit impossible among His followers; for the legal spirit seeks to establish by virtue of its righteousness some claim upon divine reward.

But does not our Lord encourage the expectation of some reward? Does He not imply that there is a reward of the Father which is in heaven? Does He not say, "Thy Father which seeth in secret shall recompense thee"? If this be so, does He not clearly hold out the thought of a reward to those who are fulfilling deeds of righteousness, and giving of their substance in aid of the needy? It is quite true that there is reward, for we live in a world where all things are ordered by an ultimately just and faithful law. And as every law means that consequences follow from actions, no man can act without meeting with the recompense of his deed. But this is not the kind of reward which the expectant religionists looked for. They thought of some recompense which bore no natural or orderly relationship to their conduct. They had no idea of a sovereignty whose love lay in its faithfulness: they thought rather of a ruler whose caprice was to be feared, and whose favour might be secured by apt and opportune homage. The character of God was not understood. They judged Him to be a respecter of persons; and they judged that His regard might be judiciously enlisted by those who were astute enough to pay the requisite price. Thus the reward they looked for was outside the range of the law of righteous consequence. The recompense our Lord had in view was the recompense which comes unsought and undesired to righteous-hearted men, and yet which comes to them as surely as the flowers spring from the soil where the seed has been sown. For it is a truth of life that reward which is least sought is the reward which is most inevitable. And this reward is the reward which the spiritually-minded most desire. The kind action, like virtue, must be spontaneous and unconscious of its own kindness (so to speak), and then its reward comes, as the reward of all exercise comes, in enlarged capacity. Character makes heaven, and character grows into magnanimous and noble proportions, or shrinks into meanness or pettiness according to our habitual lines of conduct.

> "All characters
> Must shrink or widen as our wine skins do,
> For more or less that we can pour in them."

The reward is found in the growing capacity for nobleness. Love, which is often but a casual visitor in human hearts, becomes, if we will but encourage its kindly suggestions, an abiding guest. Courage and self-forgetfulness, which are at first only occasional, become habitual. The soul becomes a nobler thing as character becomes the home, where noble virtues are domesticated and act with the force and suggestiveness of masters and friends, and no longer with the doubtfulness and timidity of guests. While this transformation is taking place the character is growing divine—more like to God, who is our exceeding joy. Our reward is one with our spiritual growth; our final satisfaction is in being like unto Him. There is reward enough in this; for the exercise of faculties, when they have become completely under our mastery, is in itself a delight. The glory and reward is not in flying fame or transient applause or earthly gain: the glory is the power, as Tennyson sang, of still going on; the reward is in the capacity of working according to the true and divine law of our being—*i.e.*, according to His will whose name is love, and whose service is perfect freedom.

There is a third corruption, that of self-consciousness or sentimentalism. Has our Lord any antidote for this? I think so. It will be noticed that our Lord insists upon the most complete simplicity in beneficence. There must be no ostentation, no straining after effect. There must be no reckoning up of the merit of the action in the esteem of the world or to our own advantage. He pushes this principle of simplicity so far home that He says even in the sphere of a man's own being there must be no measuring of the merit of his deeds. "Let not thy left hand know what thy right hand doeth." Does He not prohibit the dwelling on our own kindnesses? Does He not point out and condemn self-consciousness, self-esteem, self-satisfaction in every form or shape? All sentimental self-approval is thrust far away by such a precept as this.

What then, according to our Lord, ought to be the characteristics of true beneficence?

It ought to be too simple and manly in motive to warrant self-consciousness, or to be mere self-indulgence. It ought to be the outcome of a spirit so entirely filial that it looked for no reward, and indeed could not view any action in the light of a bargain with God, or as wrought with any thought of securing His favour. It ought to be too real in its benevolence for the presence of any motive of ostentation.

Beneficence, then, should possess the qualities of spontaneousness, thoughtfulness and affluence.

1. Beneficence should be spontaneous. It should be the inevitable outcome of a good heart. There is a quality in true poetry which Wordsworth described

by the word Inevitableness. He said of one writer's poetry that it lacked inevitableness. It is this which is so often lacking in poetry. We feel that much of it is written by a stern effort of will, or out of the compulsion of circumstances. It is written because the man willed to write a poem, or it is written to order. It is not written out of sheer spontaneous love, moved by the necessity of genius, and not by coercion of will or at the invitation of an editor. We may apply the thought to beneficence. Too often beneficence is due to the coercion of the moment, the impulse of a quickly stirred sentiment, and not the spontaneousness of a loving and responsive heart. But this spontaneousness is just what is wanted. It should be to the heart like the hue of the emerald which shines with its green beauty because it is its nature so to shine. It should be like the song of the linnet which

"Pipes because it must."

II. Beneficence should be thoughtful. It should be regulated by principle—*i.e.*, it should not be at the mercy of a mere sentiment. It should possess the element of thoughtfulness, because it should be animated by the real desire to do the best which can be done. It should not be of the cheap kind which gives a shilling to get rid of the importunity of a beggar, or to avoid the appearance of a mean disregard of the suppliant offertory bag, or to satisfy that uneasy argument of the casually beneficent—" I suppose I ought to give something." True beneficence ought to stand on a more settled principle than any of these motives imply. It ought to be a part of a man's whole life. It ought to make itself felt in the administration of his whole income. It ought not to appear only at church or when some special claim is brought before him. It ought to be an abiding principle of his life and so find a place in the system of his expenditure. It ought not to be casual, but constant. It ought not to be impulsive, but systematic.

III. Beneficence ought to be abounding and affluent. The snare of system might be the awakening of the legalistic spirit; but the safeguard against this is the possession of the filial spirit, which remembers who and what its Father is. The Father's beneficence is continuous and abounding. It falls like rain and it spreads like sunshine: it touches and glorifies everything. He who possesses this spirit will feel himself the guardian of his Father's gifts, and will administer them in the spirit of his Father. There will be system and order, but no hard-and-fast line. The stream of beneficence will gather volume as it flows. Like old Bishop Wilson's charity it will grow with increasing years. He who began by devoting a tenth, as the least a Christian man could give, will end by a generosity which gives much more because life and spirit, yea, all that he has, is consecrated to God, nay belongs to Him who is the creator and giver of all.

Such are the features of true beneficence. It is, in Christ's view, the offspring of a loving heart which bears resemblance to the Father's heart. Its love is natural, single-minded and kindly. It is thoughtful, but it has no thought of itself. It is free, yet it acknowledges the bonds which bind it to its fellow-men. It is alive, and it has in it therefore the power of growth, and in its growth it finds its own exceeding great reward; for thus it is becoming more like to Him who created it, inspired it, and made it for Himself.

THE PRAYER OF PRAYERS

St. Matt. vi. 9-13

Our Father, which art in heaven, Hallowed be thy Name. Thy kingdom come. Thy will be done in earth, As it is in heaven. Give us this day our daily bread. And forgive us our trespasses, As we forgive them that trespass against us. And lead us not into temptation; But deliver us from evil: For thine is the kingdom, The power, and the glory, For ever and ever. Amen.

THE PRAYER OF PRAYERS

THE same principle which governs our beneficence should also govern our prayers. Ostentation in almsgiving is a vice which robs charity of its virtue. Ostentation in prayer crushes out its very heart. And yet among the Jews this habit of ostentation prevailed. They loved to stand and pray in the synagogues and in the streets. There was no sin in praying in the synagogue. Our Lord Himself joined in these public services of religion. There was no sin in praying in the street. In the throng of business, and with the great stream of life flowing past him, many a saint of God has lifted up his heart to God, and found that his cares have vanished though the demands of work continued. The evil was not in prayer said in street or synagogue, but in prayer said with the vainglorious motive "that they may be seen of men" (Matt. vi. 5). It is the vice of ostentation which our Lord rebukes. And prayer, of all religious duties, least calls for such ostentation. In its deepest meaning it is the communing of the spirit with the Father of spirits. It is the cry of need, the child of felt weakness or conscious sin, the faith of the soul in Him who is great and who must be love. For this, what publicity is needed? No, rather does such a thing ask for quiet retirement. It seeks the place where the distractions are least, and where immunity from the irritating interrogations and solicitudes of life may ensure calm. But it is here that sentimental weakness might find a place. Such weakness would confess that prayer was needed and that the quiet spot apart would conduce to prayer, but it would feebly regret that in its hurrying life no such quiet could be found. Our Lord hints that we must exert some vigour of resolution to secure the calm which is needed. Many who deplore that they have no peaceful spot for prayer lack the determination to follow Christ's precept: "But thou, when thou prayest, enter into thine inner chamber, and having shut thy door, pray to thy Father which is in secret." And here it is only fair to remember that in the crowded life of our modern cities no determination could secure for those who are huddled in squalid and narrow tenements the right and power over any inner chamber which could be made the sanctuary of secret prayer. For such, perhaps, the most retired spot is the church, whose generous and kindly doors invite the tired and crowd-pressed to turn from the multitudinous street and rest and pray. But wherever it is, the prayer prayed to the Father in secret is a vital part of true religion. It is the health of the soul. No public prayers, no recited offices, can take its place. The soul which is alive must find its way to communion with its Father—the Father in secret, who knows and understands and hears—the Father who will recompense, not with any gift to satisfy the heart of covetousness nor with any largesse of favour given as though prayer were a bribe, but with that highest and best reward, the deepened sense of His nearness, the stronger conviction of His wisdom, and the abiding realisation of His love.

There is another evil which mars prayer. Ostentation in prayer is a vice which owes its existence to the thought of men and the desire of their applause, but there is an evil which comes from wrong thoughts of God. There were those in our Lord's day who regarded prayer as a sort of incantation. They failed to realise that the heart's wish was the heart of the prayer. They believed that the mechanical act of repetition had some virtue, so that though the heart went no longer with the words, the words uttered would win the boon.

Against this Christ warns His disciples as against a heathenish thought. "And in praying use not vain repetitions as the Gentiles do; for they think they shall be heard for their much speaking."

Here, again, it is not the repetition of a prayer which is condemned, for our Lord Himself in His agony in the garden repeated His prayer again and again. He "prayed a third time, saying again the same words" (Matt. xxvi. 39-44). When the heart is in the words, the words are no longer vain repetition—earnestness reiterates, emptiness repeats. The followers of Baal cry, "O Baal, hear us," from morning till evening. The multiplication of words with an absent heart is not prayer. "In this matter," says Lightfoot ("Hor. Heb.," Works, vol. ii. 145), "the Jew sinned little less than the heathen. For this was a maxim with them—Every one that multiplies prayer is heard." What Christ condemned was the vain theory that words could become substitutes for earnestness of soul. He would expose the false opinion that there was "some power, or zeal, or piety, in such kind of repetitions" ("Hor. Heb.," Works, vol. ii. 145.) "Be not, therefore, like unto them, for your Father knoweth what things ye have need of before ye ask Him." It is only true and worthy thoughts of God which will save men from these foolish and heathenish practices. If we can but think of Him as the all-wise and all-loving Father, who understands our hearts long before, and whose purpose towards us is an unswerving purpose of love, we shall not dream of imagining that empty and heartless words could avail to make Him change His wise designs, or that such an offering could be acceptable to Him who weighs the hearts of men. Thus our Lord cautions against a vice in prayer which in part owes its origin to false and low conceptions of God.

But our Lord knew also human weakness. He knew how even intelligent piety halted in its prayers, and how even honesty of spirit might tempt a man to abstain from prayer which, though hesitating, would, by its genuineness, draw him nearer to God. Knowing this, Christ gave to His disciples the pattern of prayer. "After this manner, therefore, pray ye." And then follows the prayer known for eighteen centuries as the Lord's Prayer—the prayer which, being used of all Christendom, is the prayer of four hundred millions of people to-day.

1. The Lord's Prayer contains seven petitions. In a degree these petitions reflect the thoughts of the beatitudes. It is, of course, only a petty spirit which seeks to make these petitions literally conform, as it were, to the beatitudes; but there is a

general and large agreement of thought between them. Thus the opening petition of the Lord's Prayer, like the first beatitude, takes us away from self in order to fill us with the remembrance of God. The poor in spirit, the man who has ceased from self is the man who will pray most truly, "Hallowed be Thy name." The meek who will inherit the earth can most fitly say, "Thy kingdom come." The mourner finds a blessing when he can pray, "Thy will be done." Those who hunger for righteousness have as much right and as much necessity as the physically needy to pray, "Give us this day our daily bread." The merciful who look to obtain mercy can enter as none else can enter into the meaning of the prayer, "Forgive us our debts as we also have forgiven our debtors." Well may the pure in heart who shrink from sin pray, "Lead us not—bring us not—into temptation." The peacemakers may dread the malignant power which stirs up strife and sows discord, and may cry, "Deliver us from the evil one." But these parallels must not be pressed too far. To do so is to lose the breadth and range both of the beatitudes and of the Lord's Prayer. They may, however, serve to show us that there are certain principles which our Lord reiterates and insists upon as belonging to the order of His great kingdom. The general outline of these principles is clear. It is to cease from self—to seek the kingdom within in the purification of the dispositions of the soul rather than in any outward gain or seeming—to find happiness, not in our own weak choice or in obstinate self-will, but in the doing and the bearing of God's will; in being content with divine support, and in reckoning it our best triumph when we are victorious over evil. Everywhere Christ teaches that His kingdom is spiritual. The prayer He has given us is built on this thought, for it is a prayer for spiritual victory in the hallowing of God's name, in the doing of His will, in the feeding on His food, in the resting on His forgiving love, in the deliverance from temptation and evil. There is no prayer for high estate, lofty place or large resources. It is the prayer of paradise, of the true paradise, which is truest because most inward. " Reason," says Jacob Behmen, "asks where is paradise to be found? Is it far off or near? Is it in this world or is it above the stars? Where is that desirable country where there is no death? Beloved, there is nothing nearer you at this moment than paradise, if you incline that way." And why? Because, " paradise is the divine and angelical joy, pure love, pure joy, pure gladness, in which there is no fear, no misery and no death."

II. The Prayer.

It opens with the supreme word, and with the thought which upholds all other thought—Our Father. All theology lies in this utterance, and all religion and all philanthropy also. All theology, for this is the parent truth of all divine truths that one is our Father, even God. All religion, for to realise this truth, to rest in it, to understand it spiritually as a living thought, so that we ourselves turn to this Father as indeed our Father, the fountain of all joy and the source of all wisdom, discipline, and goodness in life, is to grasp the heart of religion. All philanthropy, for to realise that the whole world may join with us in praying this prayer is to realise the brotherhood which is as eternally true as is the divine fatherhood. And lastly, to realise that this Father of ourselves and of the whole world also is the heavenly Father, is to bring to our minds the exceeding spirituality of His kingdom, the loftiness and sweet severity, as well as the matchless and divine tenderness, of His dealings with us, who seeks not so much to please us as to realise Himself in us, and so to raise us to the highest joy through the purest good.

Hallowed be Thy name.

This is the first petition. It implies that reverence for God is a first step of true life. But, naturally, this reverence is not of the lip only. It is not a prayer mainly and chiefly for the maintenance of the externals of worship. It is much deeper than this. It is for that spirit out of which all worship should spring. It is the prayer that God may be made first in all the thoughts and wishes of every man. It is the prayer that the name of God may be no empty name to which is accorded an empty homage, but that the name which stands for the reality and the character of God may be a living, holy, real thing to every one, that the living God may be enshrined in the heart of all His creatures as the first, chiefest, loveliest, holiest, and most hallowing power and thought in human life. And two things follow from this. First, God must be all, self must be nothing. How can God's name be hallowed in a life whose chief motive is self-indulgence, self-pleasing, self-will? And secondly, it implies the sanctification of the whole nature of man: since the true hallowing of God's name is that which brings about in and among men resemblance to His character. Otherwise the hallowing of the name is a thing on the surface. The hallowing of God's name, which is a real hallowing, is according to that word of Christ: "If a man love me, he will keep my saying; and my Father will love him, and we will come to him and make our abode with him."

And thus it will be seen that this first petition

gives a hue to the whole of the Lord's Prayer. It stands first; it strikes the keynote of purified human desire. God is first; and resemblance to Him man's first prayer. And all that follows is conditioned by this prayer. The kingdom which is to come, the will which is to be done, are the kingdom and the will of God whose holiness needs to be fulfilled in men. For thus the sacred writers speak: "A sceptre of righteousness is the sceptre of His kingdom" (Ps. xlv. 6). "This is the will of God, even our sanctification" (1 Thes. iv. 3). "Holiness becometh His house for ever" (Ps. xciii. 5), and men "give thanks for His name," which is not only "great and wonderful," but "holy" also (Ps. xcix. 3). Thus those who are striving against evil and fighting their bosom foe are encouraged when they think that His nature is the guarantee of their ultimate victory; and so they give thanks at the remembrance of His holiness. Thus we touch in this prayer the great ethical condition of all religion and of all victory of faith; for we are in view of that holiness without which no man shall see the Lord! The advent of the kingdom would bring no joy, unless His name were holy. The doing of His will would be but submission to power, not to that holy power which the conscience must approve. We can only pray, Thy will be done, when we know that that will is holy. When we think of our needs, it is the remembrance that He is holy which can make us bold in praying, Give us this day our daily bread, since He will ever sustain us with that which will best nourish our growth in goodness. He will feed us with no harmful diet, but with food convenient for us. His holiness also helps our prayer for forgiveness. To pray to be forgiven by a being in whom no holiness dwelt would be but a prayer to be delivered from penalties inflicted by his caprice. To pray to be forgiven by one whose name is holy is a prayer which means that we put ourselves beside His holiness in our hatred of evil, and that we are making His holiness our refuge from our own unholiness. To Him, because He is holy, we can turn for rescue from our temptations, and for deliverance from the evil one. The thought of holiness pervades the whole prayer. The spirit of the first petition is the spirit of the whole. We never let go our hold upon the ethical basis of the divine kingdom. We never forget that we live under the righteous rule of the righteous king.

Thy kingdom come.

Lightfoot mentions a Jewish axiom: "That prayer wherein there is no mention of the kingdom of God is not a prayer." The Jew looked forward to the day of Messiah's kingdom. It was his great hope; for it was to bring the golden age to his nation and great prosperity to his people. We can well understand how the thought and expectation of this kingdom found a place in every prayer. The Jew no doubt had wrong conceptions; he dreamed of the coming of God's kingdom as though it were a kingdom after the fashion of the kingdom of David or Solomon. Military triumphs and abundance of wealth figured in his imagination as features of that age. But other thoughts, purer and more spiritual, must have had a place there. "In His days shall the righteous flourish, and abundance of peace so long as the moon endureth, or till the moon be no more." So it was written in the seventy-second Psalm which gave a picture of a kingdom in which equity, justice and mercy were to be recognised. "He shall judge thy people with righteousness, and thy poor with judgment. The mountains shall bring peace to the people, and the hills in righteousness. He shall judge the poor of the people: He shall save the children of the needy. .... He shall redeem their soul from oppression and violence; and precious shall their blood be in His sight."

The same spirit of righteousness and deliverance and pity finds place in those words of the prophet: "The spirit of the Lord is upon me, because He anointed me to preach good tidings to the poor;

He hath sent me to proclaim release to the captives, and recovering of sight to the blind, to set at liberty them that are bruised, to proclaim the acceptable year of the Lord." As prophecy grew the material aspects of the kingdom became less, the spiritual aspects more and more—till Christ made it clear that the kingdom was a kingdom which was character—a kingdom not meat and drink, but righteousness, peace and joy in the Holy Ghost. The sword of this kingdom is not the sword which destroys men's bodies, but which slays their passions and saves their souls. It is the sword of the spirit which is the word of God. The weapons are not carnal. The armour is the armour of righteousness on the right hand and on the left.

When we translate this teaching into modern speech, we begin to understand that the kingdom which we pray for is the kingdom of righteousness, truth, fair dealing, generosity, pity, charity, purity. It is the kingdom in which the spirit of Christ is the law of souls. It is the kingdom, therefore, in which selfishness, meanness, dishonesty, uncleanness, injustice and unscrupulousness can have no place. It is no kingdom in which the power of God enforces itself by material means. The sword is in the mouth, not in the hand. It is the word which works by reasonable persuasion, by clear conviction, by intelligent and honest acquiescence. The kingdom of God will not have truly come as long as obedience to the laws of the kingdom is due to compulsion or mere fashion, or the fear of being thought irreligious. It only comes when all men freely and by choice live by the laws of Christ. Thus the state of things aimed at is higher than any law-enforced socialistic conception. It is rather that state wished for by Tennyson—"when all men's good (shall) be each man's rule"—and this in the highest sense—for it will be right done and good promoted for love's sake.

This kingdom would bring peace and contentment. Men would not seek to grow rich at their brother men's pain or cost. Universal tenderness and kindly consideration would everywhere prevail. Men would vie with one another in the happy rivalry of service, not in the fierce competition for wealth. Nations would distribute their produce, and no longer set barriers against the natural expansion of growing races. The law of service would so sway men's hearts and motives that littleness, trickery and fraud would be impossible. The vision lies in the future. It will surely come: it will not tarry. But it must come in natural order, and by lawful means. And therefore our Lord teaches us further to pray:

Thy will be done on earth, as it is in heaven.

For this is the way in which the kingdom is to come. It is there wherever God's will is done on earth as it is in heaven. For in heaven there is no constraint. It is the home of free activities. That which is done is that which it is gladness to do. No bondage of compulsion has place there, and therefore there is no sulky obedience or specious insincerity. In heaven the will of God is done by spirits which know and love His will. His will is the joy of their life, the law of their being; for it is the good and acceptable and righteous will of God. There love carries out the purposes of Him whose name is love.

And here we may see how very scant is the interpretation so often given to this prayer, "Thy will be done." We see it written on tombstones, we hear it sighed forth as a chastened sentiment when some great loss has been sustained, and some great bereavement has left the home desolate. It is the prayer of resignation, of gentle and soft acquiescence in some inscrutable providence. It is in this sense altogether passive. No doubt there are times when this is the sweet and utter duty of the pained and troubled soul. The dead were dear; they are dear; it has been hard to give them up, even to God. "Thy will be done." God is stronger, greater: He has taken them. He is loving too.

He does it wisely. Yes. "Thy will be done," may well be prayed then. But the prayer is much larger. It is the prayer which should brace us up to the ever-doing of His will. It should urge us to shape our lives and to discipline our motives so that we should ever be living and acting according to His will—nay, more, that we should so live with Him in thought and prayer, and study of His law, that we should understand His will and strive to make it our joy. It was thus that the Psalmist could speak of his delight in God's commandments. But the doing of His will should go even beyond this. It is only perfect when our spirits are so truly in sympathy with His spirit that we regard all life and all duty from the divine standpoint. We need to catch the spirit of His will, and bring the spirit of that will into all that we do. Our prayer should be

> "Our wills are ours, we know not how;
> Our wills are ours, to make them Thine."

So may we pray Christ's prayer, desiring that we should share His spirit, and love His will. And what is this but the prayer that in us, and in all human souls, the love of God may be shed abroad by the spirit which He gives? Then, indeed, when all are filled with that spirit of love, would His will be done on earth as it is in heaven.

But for this we need the sustenance and the

invigorating strength of heaven. And so Christ teaches us to pray:

Give us this day our daily bread.

This is a prayer which only a large-hearted faith can pray. It is just the prayer which a son can pray to a father. It asks not for a great abundance, but for enough. It says—Thou hast given me duty to do, give me adequate strength, give me the day's bread for the day's task. It asks no affluence to satisfy pride, but enough to satisfy need. It asks no dainties to satisfy desire, but bread to support strength. It is a prayer which is as temperate as it is trustful and modest. It is the prayer of a contented spirit, but yet of a spirit eager to discharge its duty. It leaves the choice of the food to the divine wisdom which knows best what to bestow. It is content that that wisdom should apportion to it its food. Like Agur it prays, Feed me with food convenient for me (Prov. xxx. 8).

What a lesson for the worldly, covetous, anxious-hearted, or ambitious is here! They are eager for riches: covetous, that they may outstrip some other in the race for wealth; anxious, for fear they may be overlooked in the distribution of honours; ambitious for glories in which they may excel other men. How can such pray, Give us this day our daily bread, when it is not this simple and sufficient fare which they desire, but more and yet more and more choice and ever-abounding fare they crave for? What a lesson for the distrustful spirit which desires to have goods laid up against the changes of the future, and cannot trust God for what has not yet been given, and is not yet needed. Sufficient unto the day is the evil thereof. Sufficient also is the food God daily gives. In our prudence as well as in our desires we need faith; for prudence may degenerate into faithless anxiety and forgetfulness of Him who holds to-morrow in His hand, and can give to us each day our daily bread.

And as is His providence for the needs of the body, so also is His care for the spiritual needs of His children. He who desires that we should grow up into His likeness feeds and sustains the growing life of the soul. Yea, He gives us Himself, exchanging His heart with ours, communicating unto us His spirit, making us partakers of His nature. And as the earnest and symbol of this, He has instituted that great memorial of His love which is also the sign that our life is indeed in Him and that it is only in Him that we can truly live. We can only live our own life by living His. And in this we affirm no new doctrine, but we recognise that old and eternal one that in Him we live and move and have our being. That which we take in the communion of His love is common bread and common wine; and yet to us it becomes divine, soul-sustaining and heavenly food. And this not by transformation of the divine into any earthly thing, but by virtue of the fact that the simplest creatures are pledges of His power and witnesses of His presence. The divine is never changed into the earthly, but the earthly is realised to be ever in the divine. There needs, therefore, no conversion of the Godhead into flesh or into bread, but the realisation of that unfailing divine presence in which are all things. And thus the common bread needs no transformation; for the life and virtue of all are in Him who sends all things to their use and purpose. And everything may minister divine help to our souls, seeing that His presence is never far from any one of us. And to this His real presence, the feast of the breaking of bread, must ever witness, giving us, instead of a needless wonder, the assurance of His changeless presence, and instead of the degradation of the divine, the glorious divine power which took the manhood into God.

But man needs more than sustenance. He who gives, must needs forgive. Our faults are no less real than our weakness. Therefore Christ teaches us to pray:

Forgive us our trespasses — our trespasses, our

sins, our debts. The neglect of service owed to God, the violations of sanctity, the transgressions of law, the outbursts of passion, the indulgence of evil temper, the envious and grudging spirit, our failures in brotherliness, our want of charity—what are they but blemishes on the life which the children of God should live? These, and whatsoever more we may know of, are sins for which we need forgiveness; for they separate us from the joy of God's presence, and the realisation of His life. In Christian life this experience is needed. It may be described as the inseparable condition of progress. The sense of sin is the sense of falling below what we might have been—what we ought to have been. There is a sadness and a self-reproach in this; but there is a sort of greatness also, since to be able to judge self and to condemn self is the sign that we are climbing above self. The self-criticism of the artist is the evidence that he is capable of advance to greater heights. The power of self-condemnation is the witness that we can appreciate and long for a holier and truer life. To be able to say, "Forgive us our sins," meaning what we say, is to be able to

> "Rise on stepping-stones
> Of our dead selves to higher things."

But our Lord adds something to this prayer for forgiveness. He teaches us not only to say, "Forgive us our sins," " but forgive us our trespasses *as we forgive them that trespass against us.*" Forgive—as we forgive. Here is the test of the reality of our prayer. Prayer for forgiveness is only real when the heart is softened with contrition, and humble with the remembrance and hatred of its fall. Such a softening brings tenderness. The resentments of life melt away. Pity takes the place of wrath.

Whittier tells how, with a chafed spirit, full of wrath and resentment, he strolled one summer Sabbath morning among

> " The green mounds of the village burial-place ;
> Where pondering how all human love and hate
> Find one sad level, till . . . . .
> Awed for myself, and pitying my race,
> Our common sorrow, like a mighty wave,
> Swept all my pride away, and trembling I forgave."

The large sense of human sorrow softened away all resentment. It is the same with the sense of the vast heavenly love which comes over us when we realise sin and the forgiveness of sin. We rise above petty grudges. We live and breathe in the large and kindly atmosphere of a divine mercy. Forgiveness of those who have harmed us becomes natural and easy. Where this spirit is not, the desire to be forgiven is only conventional and self-interested. It is not the desire to be quit of the sin. The paradox of this experience is that as we become hard in self-condemnation we become tender towards others. And again, the great, deep sense of the divine love and pity, like sunshine, melts the frost of pride, which makes forgiveness hard. So we get the measure—Forgive as we forgive. The parable of the unforgiving servant is Christ's own commentary on this petition: "Shouldest thou not have had compassion on thy fellow-servant even as I had pity on thee?"

And lead us not into temptation.

St James tells us that God does not tempt any man (James i. 13, 14). He also bade those to whom he wrote to rejoice when they fell into manifold temptations. If we distinguish the points of view, we shall feel that the apparent contradiction between the teaching of the Lord's Prayer and that of St. James disappears. St. James is thinking of those trials which come to test the quality of the Christian soldier, and which, when stoutly met, serve to develop his character. Our Lord is thinking of the giving way before it. St. James is thinking of meeting and mastering the enemy. Our Lord teaches us to pray that we be not delivered into his hands. Christ would not teach us to pray to escape the fight. In the world, He said, ye shall have tribulation (John xvi. 33). But He taught us to pray not to be captured by the power of the foe. And so He added the other prayer: "*But deliver us from the evil one, or from the evil.*"

The evil from which we ask to be delivered is the evil which demoralises; it is the spiritual evil which stains and darkens the soul; it is the ascendency of the wicked one over us. A man may fall into temptation and rise again; but he may also yield himself so to temptation as to become enlisted on the side of the evil, a willing captive to much-loved sin. Temptation so yielded to leads to a growing domination of evil. The character deteriorates. The conscience is silenced. The moral resistance is at an end. Then that which is most truly called evil gains its sway. Other things called evil, such as pain, loss, disappointment, bereavement, are not evil in themselves. They may from a certain standpoint be called good, since all things work together for good to them that love God. The cross may be the crown. We do not pray to be delivered from the cross, but only from the mighty, overmastering power of the evil spirit, which can desolate and demoralise the soul.

The prayer, as given in the Authorised Version, ends with a doxology. Lightfoot tells us that a doxology somewhat resembling this was used in Jewish worship. As the doxology and amen are not given in the parallel passage in St. Luke's gospel, Lightfoot infers that on the first occasion our Lord gave it as a prayer for public worship, and on the second, in answer to the request of His disciples, "Lord teach us to pray," as a model for private prayer. The doxology, however, and the amen are not found in the best MSS. of St. Matthew and are omitted in the Revised Version. Notwithstanding this, the doxology is beautiful and harmonious. It reminds us that the kingdom, whether we pray or pray not, is the Lord's, and that He is the Governor among the nations.

Such, then, is the Lord's Prayer. It is written for private or public use, so given to us by Christ that we may use it; but it is so to be used that we may understand it; and so to be understood by us that we may mean it, and so to be meant as by those who love it. Our spirit must be as His when we pray. We must be free from the exasperations, pettiness and resentments of the worldly aspect and feeling of life. We must be in love and charity with our neighbours. For more than all words, above all prayer is the spirit of prayer; and the spirit of prayer is that spirit of Christ which maketh intercession for us according to the will of God (Rom. viii.).

He, therefore, that would use aright even the Lord's Prayer, must seek the Lord's spirit to shed abroad the love of God in his heart.

WHAT IS PRECIOUS IN LIFE

Lay not up for yourselves treasures upon earth, where moth and rust doth corrupt, and where thieves break through and steal :

But lay up for yourselves treasures in heaven, where neither moth nor dust doth corrupt, and where thieves do not break through nor steal :

For where your treasure is, there will your heart be also.

The light of the body is the eye: if therefore thine eye be single, thy whole body shall be full of light.

But if thine eye be evil, thy whole body shall be full of darkness. If therefore the light that is in thee be darkness, how great is that darkness

No man can serve two masters: for either he will hate the one, and love the other; or else he will hold to the one, and despise the other. Ye cannot serve God and mammon.

Therefore I say unto you, Take no thought for your life, what ye shall eat, or what ye shall drink; nor yet for your body, what ye shall put on. Is not the life more than meat, and the body than raiment?

Behold the fowls of the air : for they sow not, neither do they reap, nor gather into barns; yet your heavenly Father feedeth them. Are ye not much better than they?

Which of you by taking thought can add one cubit unto his stature?

And why take ye thought for raiment? Consider the lilies of the field, how they grow; they toil not, neither do they spin:

And yet I say unto you, That even Solomon in all his glory was not arrayed like one of these.

Wherefore, if God so clothe the grass of the field, which to-day is, and to-morrow is cast into the oven, shall he not much more clothe you, O ye of little faith ?

Therefore take no thought, saying, What shall we eat? or What shall we drink ? or, Wherewithal shall we be clothed ?

(For after all these things do the Gentiles seek :) for your heavenly Father knoweth that ye have need of all these things.

But seek ye first the kingdom of God, and his righteousness; and all these things shall be added unto you.

Take therefore no thought for the morrow : for the morrow shall take thought for the things of itself. Sufficient unto the day is the evil thereof.

WHAT IS PRECIOUS IN LIFE

THERE is a snare of unreality in life. Its true purpose is often lost sight of in the desire for some secondary advantage. Man no longer works for the purpose of fulfilling his labour, but for the sake of something else which seems more profitable. He exchanges pride in workmanship for greed. He does not seek to turn out good but paying work. The chink of the coin is more pleasant in his ears than the call to perfection. Art is not pursued for art's sake, but for the sake of gain. Religion shares in this prostitution. Once it was the simple necessity of man's nature; now, it becomes a profitable fashion. Piety can win the profit of reputation and gold. It is no more the outcome of the soul's ardour; it is the vehicle of his avarice, and it has become unreal. A man gives alms, says his prayers, performs his fast, for the sake of advantage. When things are thus, religion is diverted from its proper end. A man's aims are degraded. His heart is divided. His trust in God is undermined. The advantage which is reaped without is accompanied by a deterioration within. The reputation and the purse may increase, but the character declines. The soul of man is wounded within him.

The injury is within. The outward deeds of piety, almsgiving, prayer, and fasting, are not evil in themselves. It is the worldly spirit which is to blame. The prevalence of unworthy and secondary motives vitiates the deeds of charity and piety. It will be understood, then, why our Lord so earnestly directs the attention of His disciples within. The heart can purify, and the heart can pollute every deed. The action needs to be sanctified by the motive; the gift by the altar. Now, if the true spirit of religion be the filial spirit, every action should be done as a son works for the love of his father. The religion which finds its support in worldly custom, worldly ambition, worldly gain, is not the religion which the Father of all can accept, since He looks not on the outward appearance, but on the heart. Christ seeks to enforce a religion animated by a filial spirit. He sees in the customs and practices around Him a religion which has become unreal. He sees in it a religion which is degrading instead of raising man's character. He points out the threefold degradation

—Degradation of aim; division of heart; lack of faith in God.

1. *Man's aims are degraded.*

This is the theme of the early part of Matthew vi. Christ takes the works of piety in order. He shows how almsgiving, prayer, and fasting, may be practised, not in a religious, but in a worldly spirit. He does not deny that this may be profitable; on the contrary, He admits the advantage which may accrue. He says of those who act thus, "They have their reward" (Matt. vi. 3, 5, and 16). They have their reward in the applause of men, in the increase of their reputation for liberality and piety. But such a reward can only be pleasing to a spirit which has already become deteriorated. Its desires must have fallen low. The glory of divine things, the pleasure of a Father's smile, the delight of growing into a Father's likeness, the satisfaction of being and doing that which the Father would wish, must have lost their charm. The tastes and ambitions must have become coarse and earthly. The love of this world's treasures must have taken hold of the heart.

Hence comes the caution of verse 19. "Lay not up for yourselves treasures upon the earth." The warning comes in fitly after the description of the earthly sort of religion which rested on worldly gain and applause. Christ indicates to those who follow the fashionable religion of their day that, notwithstanding all appearance to the contrary—their alms, prayers, and fasts—they are but worldlings, whose treasure is on earth and whose heart must be there also.

In pity and tenderness He reminds them of what they must very well know, that such treasure is transitory. It is exposed to the natural corruption of all earthly things. The moth and rust can destroy. Wealth and reputation wear out. It is exposed also to the rivalry and robbery of those whose interests are contrary to ours. The thieves may break through and steal (verses 19, 20). But it is the inward degradation which presses most upon our Lord's thought. No man can be thus enamoured of earthly reward or reputation without bringing his heart to this earthly level. The heart, which is the seat of religion; the heart, which might be the source of glorious and ennobling emotions; the heart is sinking into the mud of mere earthliness. It must be so; for where the treasure is, there will the heart be also (verse 21). We may test ourselves by asking, What do we love best? The whole of our nature takes its law from the heart. Our works, our thoughts, our conversation, take their tinge and tone from our hearts. The motive which animates it infects or illumines the whole of our being. "The light of the body is the eye" (verse 22).

The light of the body is the eye. The illustration is simple enough. If we close the eye, we are in darkness. If we open it to heaven's light, our whole frame partakes of the joy of that light. A pleasant thing it is to behold the sun. Every pulse, every muscle, every nerve, seems to partake of the brightness which is poured in upon the open eye. In the same way everything depends upon the purity and simplicity of motive. He is a good man whose motives and aims are good. "If, then, thine eye be single, thy whole body is full of light" (verse 22). The whole soul passes under the sway of the motive. If the heart is enlisted, then the whole of our being is brought into service. The single eye here is like the honest and good heart spoken of in the parable of the sower (Luke viii. 15). But, on the other hand, "If thine eye be evil, thy whole body is full of darkness" (verse 23). If the aim and motive be base and low, the whole nature suffers. It is as though an evil darkness spread over it. Nothing is seen in its true colours. The heart colours everything. The principle which Christ declares is one which is recognised by many writers. Sir Walter Scott in "Redgauntlet" represents Alan Fairford writing to Daisie Latimer. "All that happens to thee gets a touch of the wonderful and sublime from thine own rich imagination. Didst thou ever see what artists call a Claude Lorraine glass, which spreads its own particular hue over the whole landscape which you see through it? Thou beholdest ordinary events just through such a medium." In the bad sense the same principle is expressed in the well known lines:

> "All seems infected that the infected spy,
> As all looks yellow to the jaundiced eye."

So in the moral world. Worldly eyes see everything from a worldly point of view. The merit and value of everything is so measured. Higher considerations do not appeal to them. The eye is evil. Darkness pervades the whole nature. Heaven's light finds no entrance, or is seen only through a false tinted medium. The deterioration is complete when the organ which should be the vehicle of light is either closed to light or distorts it. "If, therefore, the light that is in thee be darkness, how great is that darkness" (verse 23).

II. *The heart is divided.*

The picture which our Lord drew in the previous verses prepares for what follows. The eye, which should give entrance to pure light, may, through perversion or disease, give only imperfect admission to it. The light suffers from the medium through which it passes. The motive of the heart perverts the vision of the soul. But man is a creature of mixed motives. The best are not wholly pure in motive. The worst are not wholly corrupt. The Pharisee, whose heart was smitten with worldliness, and whose pride was inflated with the world's applause, had no wish to be wholly irreligious. Mixed feelings governed his life. The hope that he was truly religious did not quite forsake him, even while he paid such abject homage to the world. He wished to stand well with God, while he secured the high opinion of man. His eye was not single; double desires possessed his heart: worldliness confused heaven's light. He was attempting the impossible. Against this our Lord uttered His caution, "No man can serve two masters" (verse 24).

"No man can serve two masters; for either he will hate the one, and love the other; or else he will hold to the one, and despise the other." We see the reason at once. The heart can have but one allegiance at a time. We may have many friends. We can have but one master; for the soul must have its preferences; and it will soon choose between master and master. Nay, according to our Lord's previous sayings, the soul has already chosen.

The Pharisee had given his allegiance to the world. In the world's applause and approval he found his joy. There he found, as he had sought, his reward; there was his treasure; there was his heart. The service of God, under the circumstances, was only a pretence. How could he give his heart to God, whose heart was already bound to the service of the world and whose love and whose hopes were there? No belief in our own piety can make us pious under such circumstances. No worldly approval could make us servants of God when our hearts were already given away from Him. "Ye cannot serve God and mammon" (verse 24).

The evil of this divided heart is that it really means alienation from God. It also means that the character cannot grow in unity with itself. The difference between greatness and littleness among men is found in the presence or lack of concentration. One man gives his whole soul and mind to the matter in hand, another can only give a distracted attention. In the one case the whole man is on the spot, in the other it is but a portion of the man. The one can, like a good general, concentrate his force where it is wanted, the other can gather together but a remnant of his powers. Transfer the thought to the moral nature. There are men who are ruled by one great and supreme idea. Every faculty and power is devoted to it. Such a fact gives dignity to a man's life. If the leading idea be a high and noble one, the character becomes ennobled in the pursuit of it. But when the life is ruled by no noble idea, character declines. When it is not governed by one idea it becomes forceless. To be at the mercy of one's passions is to be at the mercy of many winds. The course shaped under such circumstances will be a wandering, uncertain course. The man's life will be indecisive, profitless. His character will never knit together. He will never achieve the unity of his manhood. He will have learned little and be fit for little. There will be a constant discord in his life. Its music will be broken and unsatisfactory. The witness of the Prophet against the men of his day will be true. Their heart is divided: now shall they be found faulty (Hosea x. 2).

The worldly spirit divides the heart from God, and dissipates all force and concentration. Life is a vain attempt at impossible compromises. Ye cannot serve God and mammon. It is Christ's warning. And yet thousands still attempt the impossible. Their heart is given to the frivolity and emptiness of life, yet they cultivate the fashionable side of religious life. They will take part in a fête, in theatricals, and cafés chantants for religious or philanthropic objects. They will admire enthusiastically the picturesque exterior of religious life. They will delight in its displays. They may even go slumming. But they will not abandon their sacrifices at the altar of mammon. With their taste they appreciate religion. With their hearts they serve the world. They feel the unreality of their position. They seek to allay the reproaches of conscience by halting, spasmodic, and conventional attentions to religious claims and duties. They endeavour to reconcile the irreconcilable. They like to believe themselves pious, while their hearts are given to the world. To such Christ's words are clear and irrevocable. "No man can serve two masters. Ye cannot serve God and mammon."

Must, then, religious people go out of the world? Is the only religious life the life of the recluse and the ascetic? By no means. It is of the heart that Christ is speaking. A man may know where his heart is by asking where his treasure is. What can he the most ill afford to part with? What does he most tenaciously cling to? He will thus know which is the eye he must needs pluck out, or the hand which is better cut off. But if, indeed, he lives in the world, and its gew-gaws, and wealth, and honours are nothing to him, because he worships honour, truth, love, fidelity, purity, God, more than any of those; then wherever God's providence places him, let him use life and all that it brings in the highest service. He is in the midst of these things, but he is not betrayed by them; for his heart is otherwhere. He is like the painter or the poet who passes through the fashionable drawing-room, or the market of the city untainted, because he sees beauties which outshine all these, or hears music which is sweeter than all the sounds of earth. His heart is above these things: he is unspoiled by them—and he can live and reign among them, because his throne is placed higher than the highest which earth can understand. He whose heart is with God may live unspotted in the world. The deadly drink which poisons others he can taste without peril. He can take up the venomous beast and remain unharmed; for there is a fire of higher love into which he can cast all harmful things.

But it is not thus with all. Some must be saved by fear; the robe of worldliness must be torn off; he must hate the garment spotted by the flesh (Jude 23). Happy is he who, being crucified with Christ, is crucified also to the world. But till we are dead to the world, there is the danger that we may become demoralised and weakened by becoming worldly, and then our lives also become profitless through the vain endeavour to serve God and mammon.

III. *Trust in God is undermined.*

When the heart is fixed intently upon worldly advantage, it slowly but surely loses its trust in God. Secondary means are considered. The spirit of ambition and the arts of management take possession of the soul. The superintending wisdom of God is forgotten; the fatherly love is lost sight of. Anxiety born of over eagerness fills the heart. The jealousies, the heartburnings, the cares of the worldly life become our portion. We cannot leave things in God's hands. We lose faith, for the childlike spirit is no longer ours. That priceless gift has been lost. In its place comes a load of earthly anxieties. Hence our Lord gives this counsel: "Take no thought (or rather, Be not anxious) for your life, what ye shall eat or what ye shall drink; nor yet for your body, what ye shall put on. Is not the life more than the food, and the body than the raiment? Behold the birds of the heaven; for they sow not, neither do they reap, nor gather into barns; yet your heavenly Father feedeth them. Are ye not much better than they?" (verses 25, 26). Thus our Lord leads His hearers back to the simple life of childlike trust. In being worldly, He seems to say, you have gathered anxieties which are inconsistent with the filial spirit. If you realise the heavenly Father, you will not need to be the victim of such anxious cares. To understand His love is to be at rest about the future. The terrible to-morrow, which casts its heavy shadow upon so many hearts, need never darken yours—for your heavenly Father, who feeds the birds, deems you much better than they.

The connection needs to be observed. The link between verse 24 and 25 is very strong. The divided life is vain. Ye cannot serve God and mammon. Therefore—on this very ground—I say unto you, "Be not anxious for your life," &c. The anxious spirit is a sign that the mammon power rules the heart. It is not the rich man only who is a worldling. The poor man who is the prey of gnawing misgivings betrays the power which the world has over his soul. In the struggle of existence the eyes of men—rich and poor alike—are drawn too much to the things that perish. The rich who cling to their wealth and the poor who grasp at it practically say that a man's life does consist in the abundance of the things possessed. To such the meat is more than life; the raiment more than the body. "Having food and raiment, let us therewith be content" (1 Tim. vi. 8), is in their view a text for philosophers who are enamoured of their studies and who ask no more than strength of body and mind to continue them. The quiet peace which faith in a Father's love can bring, cannot be the portion of those who cherish discontent. Feverish and greedy impatience destroys trust. The anxiety to increase material possessions springs from the same parentage as the miserliness which hoards them. The craving for more pierces the soul through with many sorrows (1 Tim. vi. 10).

"Take no thought," says our Lord. Does He, then, check the impulses of prudence? Is thrift inconsistent with the heavenly spirit? Not so; our Lord is not thinking of the calm and prudent spirit which endeavours by a wise forethought to prevent himself or his children becoming a burden to others. A man is bound to provide for his own (1 Tim. v. 8). The law, which bids us do to others as we would they should do unto us, sanctions this proper provision for our own. The self-denial which seeks to avoid being burdensome to others is but a part of brotherly love. Our Lord by no means sanctions that heedless selfishness which is content to enjoy itself and leave the burden of to-morrow to others. He only chides the feverish, worldly spirit, which frets and harasses itself with needless fears and greedy anxieties. He would say, do your duty to-day. Act with courage, diligence, and prudence to-day. Do not fret after the impossible. Do not give way to the spirit which desires to be something which God has not made you. Play the game according to the rules. Do your best with the tools which have been given you. No anxiety can alter the conditions of life. "Which of you by taking thought can add one cubit to his stature?" (verse 27). We may improve the conditions of life by industry and foresight. This is to use the talents God has given. To be the victim of restless desires and burning discontent is as wrong as it is useless. It tends to despondency, indolence, or dishonour. Because we have only one talent, we are not therefore justified in wrapping it in a napkin and doing nothing. The men of Chitral did not lay down their arms because their forces were scant and their difficulties many. They did not vainly fret; but they planned prudently and fought bravely. They did their best with such resources as they had. They were not the victims of fretful, feverish anxiety. This had unnerved them. So would Christ have His soldier to fight, courageously and thoughtfully—not conjuring up new fears, but facing present difficulties, mindful of the love which never fails and of the eye which never sleeps.

Every care may be cast upon God, when every duty is being manfully done. St. Peter gave the counsel "Casting all your care upon Him." He used the same word which our Lord uses here. Care in the sense of fretful, distracting anxiety should have no place in the heart of the true son of God—for He (God) careth (the word is different now: it has no touch of fever or distress in it) for you (1 Pet. v. 7).

All disturbing, anxious care may go. We may rely upon our Father, if we are doing fitly His will. There need be no anxious thought for food: He feeds the birds; nor yet for raiment: He clothes the lilies in their splendid hues. "Verily I say unto you that even Solomon in all his glory was not arrayed like one of these. Wherefore, if God so clothe the grass of the field, which to-day is, and to-morrow is cast into the oven, shall He not much more clothe you, O ye of little faith?" (verses 29, 30).

We sometimes hear language which implies, if it does not say, that our Lord here counselled impossibilities. If the world, it is said, were to act upon Christ's advice, it would be ill for the world. Men would go without the necessities of life. But we have seen that our Lord does not forbid thrift and prudence, but only that worldly-minded anxiety that cannot do its duty to-day without peering curiously and fearfully into the face of to-morrow. He is only the foe of distracting and needless care. But further, He recognises the ordinary needs of life. If He counsels us against this troubled anxiety, He declares that the heavenly Father recognises ordinary human needs. "Therefore"—such are His words—"take no thought, saying what shall we eat, or what shall we drink, or wherewithal shall we be clothed? (for after all these things do the Gentiles seek) for your heavenly Father knoweth that ye have need of these things" (verses 31, 32). Ye have need of all these things, and your heavenly Father knoweth it. He does not counsel idleness. He worked with His hands, giving us an example that we should follow His steps; but He worked as always under the care of the heavenly Father; and He would make us partakers of His spirit, that we might never doubt the Father's love, or imagine that He did not know that we have need of all these things. "The hand of the diligent maketh rich," said the Old Testament writer, remarking on the success which attends industry (Prov. x. 4). Let him work with his hands that he may have to give to him that needeth, said the apostle, remarking on the use of wealth (Eph. iv. 28). And our Lord gave no counsel which is hostile to the industry thus inculcated. He rather thought of the spirit in which life and work should be faced. He sought to banish the anxious care which grew out of forgetfulness of the Father's love. He sought to banish it also, because it was a sign that the heart had forgotten the higher in its eagerness for the lower.

Wherever this care existed, the true aim of life was obscured. The heavenly Father and the Father's kingdom were lost sight of; and therefore He closed this section of the Sermon by bringing back the thoughts of His disciples to this supreme end of life. Do not give way to anxious care, but "seek ye first the kingdom of God and His righteousness." We are taken back to the language with which the Sermon opens—the first benediction told of the kingdom of heaven. It was to be the portion of those who sought not their own. It belonged to the poor in spirit. It was the first of Christ's blessings. For this indeed is the highest blessing of the sons of men, viz., that they should realise that they belong to no earthly kingdom. The life which is circumscribed by the realm of earthly things is not worthy of those who are sons of the Father of spirits. The sons of God must realise the divine order. The sons of God must seek the heavenly kingdom. And therefore Jesus Christ, having pointed out the grave defects of the unreal religion which prevailed among the pietists of His day, urges on His disciples the supreme duty of making the kingdom—the heavenly kingdom—first in their thoughts and first in their aims. Seek ye first the kingdom; but realise that this kingdom is not material or temporal. Its pomp is not the pomp of earth. Its might is not that which the world counts might. Seek the kingdom, but seek it with the remembrance of that which constitutes its glory and its stength. Seek the kingdom and the righteousness of Him who is its King.

Righteousness, said the wise man, exalteth a nation (Prov. xiv. 34). How high and exalted then must that kingdom be whose very laws are righteousness and whose king is the Lord our righteousness! The world is slow to believe it, but it is notwithstanding true, that righteousness is the strongest thing upon earth. St. Jerome accounted justice as the mother of all virtues. He was right, seeing that without justice there could be no virtue. So in the strongest monarchy of all it is said—"A sceptre of righteousness (or uprightness) is the sceptre of Thy kingdom. Thou hast loved righteousness and hated iniquity, therefore God, even Thy God, hath anointed Thee with the oil of gladness above Thy fellows" (Ps. xlv. 6, 7, and Heb. i. 8, 9). Joy and triumph of the highest sort waits on the righteous King. His exaltation is above His fellows, because He loved righteousness; and His joy is as His exaltation. The language of our Lord is similar. It embodies for His disciples the same principle.

Fulness of joy and success wait upon righteousness. Seek first the kingdom and His righteousness; and all these things shall be added unto you (verse 33).

But is this true? Do the lovers and followers of righteousness gain all these things? Is it not the witness of the sacred writer that they wandered about in sheepskins and goatskins, being destitute, afflicted, tormented? (Heb. xi. 37, 38). And was not this because they sought first the kingdom and the righteousness? They showed the world indeed that there was a treasure more precious than all which the world held dear. But did they win these other things? They had what God saw fit and best. They were fed with the food which was most convenient for them. This was enough for them; for thus they showed that man doth not live by bread alone, but by every word that proceedeth out of the mouth of God; and they realised thus the great and spiritual glory of God's kingdom. And if more be needed, they became possessors of all things earthly, as they held the heavenly key which explained all things. Their possession was as wide as their knowledge of God (1 Cor. iii. 22). They possessed all things, because they drew from all things their true message and virtue. For them all things worked together for good (Rom. viii. 28); and so in the very truest sense all things were theirs. Every day brought its message, and its discipline of sorrow or of joy. Their faith led them to learn of each day its own message, and to accept its discipline; they were content to leave the future; they saw the work of God before them every day; they did it, regardless of anything which the future might bring. They gained all that God meant them to gain. Was not the best of heritages theirs? Were not all other things added to them?

"Take therefore no thought for the morrow; for the morrow shall take thought for the things of itself. Sufficient unto the day is the evil thereof" (verse 34).

Care adds the evil of to-morrow to the discipline of to-day. Care therefore cries, "My burden is greater than I can bear." Faith meets the pain, loss, or difficulty which is measured out to it to-day. Faith has no to-morrow's burden; for it leaves to-morrow in the hands of God. It therefore learns to say, "I can do all things through Christ which strengtheneth me; for nothing has been too heavy, neither pain, nor loss, nor temptation. All has been meted out as I was able to bear it. The strength was sufficient for the day; and out of the evil I gained the good. Thus the blessing of each day was mine."

PROSTITUTED ZEALOTISM

Judge not, that ye be not judged.

For with what judgment ye judge, ye shall be judged: and with what measure ye mete, it shall be measured to you again.

And why beholdest thou the mote that is in thy brother's eye, but considerest not the beam that is in thine own eye?

Or how wilt thou say to thy brother, Let me pull out the mote out of thine eye; and, behold, a beam is in thine own eye?

Thou hypocrite, first cast out the beam out of thine own eye; and then shalt thou see clearly to cast out the mote out of thy brother's eye.

Give not that which is holy unto the dogs, neither cast ye your pearls before swine, lest they trample them under their feet, and turn again and rend you.

Ask, and it shall be given you; seek, and ye shall find; knock, and it shall be opened unto you:

For every one that asketh receiveth; and he that seeketh findeth; and to him that knocketh it shall be opened.

Or what man is there of you, whom if his son ask bread, will he give him a stone?

Or if he ask a fish, will he give him a serpent?

If ye then, being evil, know how to give good gifts unto your children, how much more shall your Father which is in heaven give good things to them that ask him?

Therefore all things whatsoever ye would that men should do to you, do ye even so to them: for this is the law and the prophets.

Enter ye in at the strait gate: for wide is the gate, and broad is the way, that leadeth to destruction, and many there be which go in thereat:

Because strait is the gate, and narrow is the way, which leadeth unto life, and few there be that find it.

PROSTITUTED ZEALOTISM

OUR LORD has warned His disciples of the evil of unreal religion. He has shown them that when men cultivate religion for the sake of human applause, or for personal gain, they may win reward, but they demoralise their character: they make it earthly: and with lowered nature come lower conceptions of God.

But this is not the only snare to which religion is exposed. Even zeal for religion has its snares. A man may be sincere in his convictions, and yet may violate the first principles of religion. Religiosity, if we may use such a word, takes the place of real religion when a man is so enamoured of his own views, and so zealous in their defence, that he acts irreligously, *i.e.*, wrongfully, towards those who differ from him. It is against this irreligious religiosity that our Lord cautions His disciples in this closing chapter. The thought of this danger runs throughout it, though other subjects, such as self-denial, prayer, and stability of character are treated of.

Our Lord commences by warning against false judgments, which is the earliest form of this overbearing religious zeal. Fanaticism cannot differ from a person without condemning him. It is so impatient and wrathful that it begins to malign him. He is "unsound;" he holds dangerous views; his opinions are corrupt; "his character, well, what can you expect from one who advances such opinions?" Judge not is our Lord's command. It is a noble and safe law. It is right and well that we should maintain with all zeal and earnestness what we believe to be true. We have a right, nay, duty lays it upon us, to contend for truth, or what seems to us to be true; for in this way will truth be advanced. But to judge belongs to God alone. It is clear that our Lord is not speaking of the exercise of our judgment in matters of opinion. He welcomed this, as He taught men to seek for truth. He appealed to men to use their judgment. "Why even of yourselves judge ye not what is right?" (St. Luke xii. 57). Neither does our Lord forbid the exercise of legal judgment. He Himself respected it, and declared that all responsible office came from God (John xix. 11). These judgments, which are the due exercise of our natural powers, Christ did not condemn. The judgment which He forbade was the evil judgment of the passion and the prejudice which judged the man, which pretended to know all about him, and to see the moral turpitude which lurked behind mistaken opinions. It is of the uncharitable judgment and of the fanatical condemnation of men which our Lord is thinking when He says " Judge not."

This habit of judging and condemning people introduces an evil custom into society. Society is fundamentally the great brotherhood of life, bound by the ties of companionship in frailty, joy, sorrow, and experience. The pleasure and the profit of social life depend upon the sweetness and wholesomeness of its customs. If differences of opinion can be maintained with frank intelligence and with charitable spirit, then the intercourse of society will be happy and advantageous. But where a sour suspiciousness broods over every intellectual divergence the joy of social life is clouded. The harsh judgment and the eager condemnation provoke retaliation. The bigot judges the fanatic, and the fanatic condemns the bigot. A vicious system of retaliatory judgments is kept up. Varieties of mind, which might have brought much mutual profit, are made reasons for fear and alienation. Doubt and estrangement lead to hostility. Human society, which God intended to be a brotherhood of happy helpfulness, degenerates into an assemblage of men and women filled with unreasoning prejudice and ill-concealed malice. Judge not, says Christ, and He adds, that ye be not judged; condemn not that ye be not condemned; for the law of retribution is written large over the world. He that takes the sword perishes with the sword; and he that makes of his tongue a sharp sword must be slain in like manner.

There is a better occupation for men than that of judging and condemning one another. Better far it is to sit in judgment on ourselves. It is a wiser and more profitable thing to look to our own defects and to remedy these; for, strange and even paradoxical as it may seem, the purer and higher the character, the less harsh is our judgment of others, and the more capable do we become of taking our part in promoting their improvement. This thought our Lord expresses by a brief parabolic saying: "Why. beholdest thou the mote that is in thy brother's eye, but perceivest not the beam that is in thine own eye? Either how canst thou say to thy brother, Let me pull out the mote that is in thine eye, while thou thyself beholdest not the beam that is in thine own eye? Thou hypocrite; cast out first the beam that is in thine own eye, and then shalt thou see clearly to pluck out the mote that is in thy brother's eye."

PROSTITUTED ZEALOTISM

The contrast between the mote and the beam is the contrast between the small and the large. The contrast is perhaps better expressed by the splinter and the beam—the small fragment of wood and the large. It is an absurd thing for a man whose sight is impaired by a huge piece of wood to undertake the delicate operation of removing a tiny splinter which is troubling his brother's eye. But the climax of the absurdity is the idea of such a man thinking that he can do it. It is ludicrous to think of such a man being so entirely ignorant of his own defect, as to volunteer, with an air of superiority, to do the thing which requires the greatest steadiness of hand and clearness of vision to accomplish. How could such a one attempt such a task without injuring the eye which he pretends to treat? It is just this ignorant and reckless spirit which waits upon narrow fanaticism. Ill-regulated zeal judges without reflection and acts without charity. It is so fierce that it loses tenderness and consideration. It sees only the evil or error against which it is vehement. It forgets or disregards the man and his welfare. It ends by blinding him whose sight it affects to restore. Men possessed by such a spirit harm rather than help. They are of the same spirit as those of whom Christ spoke later: they would " compass sea and land to make one proselyte, and they make him tenfold more the child of hell than themselves." They impair his already feeble sight; they imbue him with their own ferocious fanaticism; they make him a fierce, blind, blundering, and malignant partisan. Such is the ruin they achieve. And how could it be otherwise, since they who put their hands to this work are so unfit for it? The beam is in their own eye. Their own power of clear vision has been already injured. That priceless gift of fair and single-minded judgment has been perverted. The eye which when it is single fills the whole body with light, has been ruined by coarse passion and fierce pretence of orthodoxy.

We thus approach verse 7, a verse which we shall most surely misunderstand unless we keep carefully in mind the drift of our Lord's argument. He is showing how the impartiality and charity of judgment can be destroyed when men judge by passion and prejudice. These hot animosities make havoc of the powers of judgment. Then He says: "Give not that which is holy to the dogs, neither cast ye your pearls before swine, lest they turn again and rend you." The usual meaning assigned to these words makes them a warning against putting holy teaching before those who are too corrupt or too degraded to understand it. It then reads like a caution to the disciples not to speak of the Gospel or heavenly things before those who are unfit to appreciate them.

But this sense makes the verse abrupt and irrelevant. It comes as a sudden interruption of the flow of Christ's teaching. It further introduces a sentiment which is little in harmony with our Lord's spirit and custom. He spoke freely of the kingdom of heaven, and He bade His disciples preach to every creature. None were too low or too degraded for the reach of heaven. The holy helps of God were given freely, as the love of God was boundless. Christ would not enjoin on any of His followers to sow the good seed with niggard or grudging hand.

The true meaning of the verse becomes clear when we allow our thoughts to move on with the flow of Christ's teaching. He gives warning, as we have seen, against the fierce and injurious influence of passion. This, like a wild creature, may seize and mangle the powers of reason and judgment. Passion may pervert judgment.

In other words, our Lord reminds us that our judgment is liable to misdirection and misuse. To enforce this He uses three illustrations. The eye may be spoilt by the beam; that which is holy may be destroyed by the dogs; and the pearl may be trampled under foot by the swine. That which the beam is to the eye, the dogs are to the holy things, and the swine are to the pearl. The gross elements destroy the finer; the beam ruins the power of sight, as the dog and the swine destroy what is precious and holy. Now the precious and holy thing is the power of just and right judgment. To be able to use our judgment with well-balanced impartiality undisturbed by passion is to exercise one of the highest prerogatives of man; but this high prerogative is open to danger. There are evils which may assail it; the sacred power may be left at the mercy of what is lower and baser. Fierce prejudice may destroy the sanctity of reason, and wild passion may disturb our reverence in the use of so priceless a thing. Prejudice, envy, indolence—these and countless more are the foes of reasonable and righteous judgment. When, then, a man allows his judgment to be at the mercy of his passion, he throws the holy thing to the dogs, he leaves the precious pearl at the mercy of the swine.

It is one of the truisms of philosophy that there is nothing so difficult to secure as the dry light of reason. The light is generally dimmed by the mists of passion, prejudice, or indolence. Bacon discourses largely and widely of the "idols" which hindered the justice and the impartiality of man's reason. "The reflection from glasses so usually resembled to the imagery of the mind, every man knoweth to receive error and variety both in colour, magnitude and shape, according to the quality of the glass. But yet no use hath been made of these and many the like observations to move men to search out, and upon search to give true cautions of the native and inherent errors in the mind of man, which have coloured and corrupted all his notions and impressions." ("Of the Interpretation of Nature.") In our own day Herbert Spencer has pointed out that all classes of men are liable to some bias, and that this bias interferes with the sobriety and safety of their judgment. In the language of the prophet, judgment goes lame, and is turned out of the way. What the philosophers thus discoursed about, the experience of men will ratify. We know well that we do not always fully appreciate the good done by people with whom we have no political or religious sympathy. The keen eye of prejudice sees evil in the good; envy and prejudice, like evil dogs, bite and maim the impartiality of our minds. We applaud charity when it is done by our own party; we deride or distrust it when it comes from the opposite camp. What is this but allowing our judgment to be at the mercy of our dislikes? Thus does some lower passion trample down the priceless gift of reason.

It is sad that after this fashion our intellectual judgment should be warped by our passions, but it is worse when we find that our moral judgments may suffer in the same way. We sometimes think that though our intellects may be wrong, our consciences must be right; but it is unfortunately only too true that the conscience, like the mind, may be made the victim of prejudice. The late Professor Mozley drew the picture of the Pharisaic conscience, as a conscience "pacified, domesticated, brought into harness—a *tame* conscience, converted into a manageable and applauding companion, vulgarised, humiliated and chained." And it was this dangerous and degraded condition that our Lord had in mind when He declared that the time would come when men's consciences would applaud the breaking of the moral law. "The time cometh that whosoever killeth you will think that he doeth God service" (St. John xvi. 2). And it is not difficult to see how this state of feeling arises. There is some evil custom or wrong belief which we are anxious to abolish. Our consciences are oppressed because such evil is tolerated; it is in our eyes a thing hateful to God and injurious to man. We reason that it cannot be wrong to get rid of evil. We therefore throw the whole of our energy and our enthusiasm into the work of annihilation; we forget everything but the desolating evil which we would fain attack. We forget to do justly by the men who are mixed up in the matter. For them we have no charity. In our eagerness to get rid of the accursed thing we act unrighteously towards our fellow-men.

We forget that men may be entangled in beliefs and customs and yet be comparatively free from moral blame. They have grown up in a different moral and religious atmosphere; they have not had perhaps the same advantages as ourselves. But our eagerness is blind to all these facts, and even injustice itself seems to be consecrated by our good intentions. The history of the world and, alas! of the Church also, will afford us many examples.

> "Urged by ambition, who with subtlest skill
> Changes her means, the Enthusiast as a dupe
> Shall soar, and as a hypocrite can stoop,
> And turn the instruments of good to ill."

Saintly men have been blinded by their fanatical zeal, and in their zeal to vindicate the honour of Christ have inflicted injustice in His name. Their deeds, as Browning said,

> "spit at their creed,
> Who maintain Him in word, but defy Him in deed."

When these things take place, that holy thing, the judgment, has been at the mercy of unholy prejudices and tumultuous passions. We can understand now, if we reflect, the significance of the words of Christ, "Neither cast ye your pearls before swine, lest they turn again and rend you." The men who, urged by furious fanaticism, have stirred up persecution against others are ever the victims of their own frenzy. They suffer at the teeth of the wild passions they have let loose. Those who have been persecuted are not the greatest sufferers; their goods were confiscated, their bodies were given to the sword or to the flame; but their persecutors suffered a loss greater than the loss of property and life, for the passions aroused in such ill work made havoc of the consciences and characters of those who indulged them. No man allows his zeal to lead him astray from the laws of God without suffering moral deterioration. Once the dogs of passion get loose they tear away the protections of our moral life; we lose by degrees our powers of fairness, impartiality, and charity. The single-mindedness of our hearts forsakes us. We wander further and further from the mind of Christ, for His ministry was not to destroy but to save. He knew the dangers into which even zeal might lead men; and He cautioned His disciples against embarking on work of destruction. The tares might be in the field, but they were to be allowed to grow together till the harvest. In the time of harvest, He said that the Lord would say to the angels, "Gather together the tares in bundles to burn them." Our dim eyes and rough hands might blunder in such work. It needs an angel eye to discern between the evil and the good, and it needs the Christ-like heart to perceive that the smoking flax may be kindled into the bright flame, and that the broken reed may be repaired and restored to form and use, and so become an instrument of heaven's music (Matt. xii. 20).

Our Lord thus teaches the principle of true judgment. Abstain from judging men, judge rather yourself. There may be a beam which spoils our own vision; it needs a very clear eye and a very delicate hand to cast the mote out of our brother's eye. When we view the evil that is in our brother we may be led away by an excess of zeal. Some earthly feeling, some unheavenly passion, may easily mingle with our judgment. The pearl of justice and charity may be flung beneath the feet of our lowest passions. Our brother may suffer at our hands, but we shall suffer that worst injury—moral deterioration. Christ teaches us that to be religious in the higher and better sense is no easy thing. Zeal for religion may be an irreligious thing, and enthusiasm for good not always good enthusiasm. We may be tempted to do evil that good may come. This is the last danger, perhaps the worst, of men and Churches. When they wake from indifference into zeal their zeal carries them beyond the commands of God. They become incapable of seeing that it can never be right, in seeking to do right, to do wrong to men.

To do this is not merely to do a moral wrong. It is an act of the supremest disbelief; for if the moral laws be indeed God's laws, then to think that good may be promoted by the violation of those laws is to say that God has given us laws which in our judgment will not work. We need, as T. T. Lynch said, "a conscience to keep our conscience." We need to remember that though wrong can never be rightly done, right may be done wrongly. Thus Christ puts before us the snares which wait upon religious profession.

Does He point out any protection against these snares? He does; His next words supply them. "Ask, and it shall be given you; seek, and ye shall find; knock, and it shall be opened unto you" (verse 7). We can trace the current of thought. Christ showed the difficulties which beset the path of religious zeal; and He reminded His disciples that all through their lives, even in the hours when their enthusiasm was greatest, they would need the quiet and sanctifying influence of prayer. The more a man grows in devotion, the more, perhaps, he needs to watch and pray. For it is hard to believe that zeal for good can lead us into evil, and that our enthusiasm for right may not be a righteous enthusiasm. It is possible, however, to be zealous in promoting God's kingdom without remembering

His righteousness. But the moment we enter the shrine of prayer we are surrounded by another atmosphere. Then we realise our weakness. We express our needs. We are conscious that our best things need purification. Our greatest strength is felt to be but weakness. Our ideas rise; our religious life is more than the pursuit of religious things; it is a self-watchful, wholesome, robust religious spirit working in all things; it is a life lived in God. In seeking the kingdom of God it seeks His righteousness.

And here, as always, our Lord draws the minds of His disciples back to the thought of the Father's love. No needy, no blinded soul can seek His face in vain. Every one that asketh receiveth, and he that seeketh findeth; and to him that knocketh it shall be opened (verse 8). And the reason of this large and ready response is to be found in the lovingness of the Father.

At this point in His sermon Christ argues in that fashion which in modern days would be called anthropomorphic. He argues from what man is to what God must be. "What man is there of you who, if his son shall ask him for a loaf, will he give him a stone? or if he shall ask for a fish, would he give him a serpent? If ye, then, being evil, know how to give good gifts unto your children, how much more shall your Father which is in heaven give good things to them that ask Him?" (verses 9–11).

We are justified then, according to our Lord, in looking into the depths of our own heart to find the outlines of the divine heart. The love, the instinctive and natural love of the father to the child, is a picture of the greater love of the greater Father. Men are fathers because God was first a father; their fatherhood is but the expression and the interpretation of His; God's message comes to us through the revelations of the natural ties of life. The God whom Christ reveals is not one that sits afar off, heedless of the pain, the misery, and the despair of His creatures, deaf to their cries and disdainful of their distress, but He is the Father who acknowledges the right of their claim to His care and His love. As their needs rise His benevolence responds. He meets their higher as well as their lower needs. If the earthly father is prompt to feed his hungry child, how much more will not the heavenly Father feed those who are hungering for Him and thirsting for His righteousness?

Christ's next words show that He has not forgotten the snares of religious zeal of which we have spoken. He teaches men that in their zeal they should not forget the charitable habit expressed by the saying, "Put yourself in his place." It is by this exchange of places that love understands many things. And therefore our Lord says: "All things, whatsoever ye would that men should do unto you, even so do ye also unto them, for this is the law and the prophets" (verse 13).

The difficulty with which Christ has been dealing is the difficulty of maintaining our religious enthusiasm alongside of our reverent allegiance to God's law. It is the difficulty of playing the game of life rightly. The petulant child grows angry with his toys, often because he does not understand or lacks the patience to obey some natural law; and even the religious man grows impatient with life because he lacks the patience to live and act under the moral laws of God. He would like to sweep the enemies of God from the earth. Christ draws him back from these passionate feelings, first by pressing on him the thought of what God is, and then by the thought of what man is. If you would but think of God, He seems to say, the power of wild passion and furious impatience would pass away. If you would think of man, you would see that he is entitled to the same charity which you claim for yourself. If God is patient with evil, should not we be? If we look for kindly treatment and kindly judgment at our brother's hands, ought we not to give him the same? If we are alive to God's holiness we shall rest upon His laws of righteousness and love; and, instead of seeking to alter or disregard them, we shall rather ask from Him strength to keep us loyal to them. It is not enough to labour to promote God's glory; we must promote it in God's way.

The temptation which constantly recurs in life is to make religion easy. But the path of religion cannot be other than narrow. For he who would follow God must not only love Him with all his heart, but with all his soul and mind also. He must love Him, that is to say, with the complete apprehension of a spirit which is earnest to be like Him in all things; and we must therefore reverence that character of God which is expressed in the moral law. We must keep this law even when it seems to put a check upon our religious zeal. But men, even earnest men, do not always realise the wide and deep application of the divine laws. They too often, in one way or another, seek to make the path of religion easier than God has made it. They open the door to the worldly spirit. And this may be done either by the pursuit of worldly aims or by reliance on unrighteous and carnal means of promoting what are called religious principles. Are we surprised, then, that Christ's next caution should be against the broad way and the wide gate?

"Enter ye in by the narrow gate, for wide is the gate and broad is the way that leadeth to destruction, and many be they that enter in thereby. For narrow is the gate and straitened is the way that leadeth unto life, and few be they that find it."

Narrow indeed is the gate, because he who enters must leave himself behind; straitened is the way, for he who seeks it must walk by faith in the divine laws, and must part with his weakness, his impatience, his prejudice. "Few," says Christ, "be they that find it." And His words are echoed by the reiterated complaint made, not in our own day, but in all generations of Christendom. The Christians are many, but where is the Christianity? Many bear the name of Christ, but do not see that the religion of Christ first demands the Christ-like character. And the Christ-like character is the character which does good and seeks no fame; which does kindness for love's sake; which is kind to the unthankful and to the unholy; which blesses and helps the unworthy; which loves all men, seeing that all men are the children of God; and which, therefore, cannot think that even in religion's name it can be good to act unkindly or to deal unrighteously by any one.

To win such a character as this all of self must be left behind. Not only our gains and possessions must we forsake, but even ourselves, as St. Augustine said. We must give up our own will and our own way. Christ must be followed in the spirit of Christ. We must be His only and His wholly. It is thus through Him that we enter into His kingdom. He is the door, and He is the way. And though this way is open to all, yet few love Him enough to give up all for His sake, and few believe in Him enough to trust themselves wholly in His hands and to shape their lives wholly by the laws of His spirit.

THE TESTS OF LIFE

Beware of false prophets, which come to you in sheep's clothing, but inwardly they are ravening wolves.

Ye shall know them by their fruits. Do men gather grapes of thorns, or figs of thistles?

Even so every good tree bringeth forth good fruit; but a corrupt tree bringeth forth evil fruit.

A good tree cannot bring forth evil fruit, neither can a corrupt tree bring forth good fruit.

Every tree that bringeth not forth good fruit is hewn down, and cast into the fire.

Wherefore by their fruits ye shall know them.

Not every one that saith unto me, Lord, Lord, shall enter into he kingdom of heaven; but he that doeth the will of my Father which is in heaven.

Many will say to me in that day, Lord, Lord, have we not prophesied in thy name? and in thy name have cast out devils? and n thy name done many wonderful works?

And then will I profess unto them, I never knew you: depart from me, ye that work iniquity.

Therefore whosoever heareth these sayings of mine, and doeth them, I will liken him unto a wise man, which built his house upon a rock:

And the rain descended, and the floods came, and the winds blew, and beat upon that house; and it fell not: for it was founded upon a rock.

And every one that heareth these sayings of mine, and doeth them not, shall be likened unto a foolish man, which built his house upon the sand:

And the rain descended, and the floods came, and the winds blew, and beat upon that house; and it fell: and great was the fall of it.

THE TESTS OF LIFE

VERY fitly does the warning against false prophets follow the picture of the strait gate and the narrow way; for the false prophets have been busy always in broadening that which God made strait and in narrowing that which He made wide. For our Lord declared that heaven was near and accessible and that in it there was room enough for all; but the heaven of the false prophets is a narrow and limited place. And yet again the false prophets break down the sideposts of the gateway of heaven and make wide that which Christ made narrow. The false prophets make much of words, and little of deeds, reversing Christ's order; for whereas our Lord said, "By their fruits ye shall know them," the false prophets say, "By their opinions ye shall know them." Our Lord said, "No man that can do a miracle in my name can lightly speak evil of me." But the mistaken and officious disciple forbids the work of such a man, "because he followeth not us."

"To follow us" is the test of faith which the foolish and the false prophets set up; to follow Christ is the Master's test. To say our shibboleth is the all-important matter with the false prophet. To bear a Christ-like character, to live a Christ-like life, full of Christ-like deeds, is all in Christ's eyes.

And, indeed, if we will reflect, this last makes the gate strait indeed to those who are entering in. He who will enter in by the door into life must needs find the gate a strait one, seeing that Christ is the door. To enter in is to be one with Christ in disposition, desire, and deed. He cannot take much with him who enters in at that door. There are many who seek to enter in, and who cannot, because they bring so many bundles with them. "Lord," they say, "let me in, but let me bring my ambition with me. It is such a little one, and there is no harm in it. Thou wilt not gainsay it." But the Lord will have no burdens brought in. All must be left outside. Heaven is worth the whole of a man's love; and Christ will have the whole of our hearts. All competing affections must be left behind. Whosoever cometh must forsake all that he hath. His earthly wealth must be as nothing to him. The things which he once held in high esteem must have no more charm for him. He must view them as dross, that he may win Christ (Phil. iii. 8, 9).

But is not this harsh? Is it not hard that Christ should so make narrow the gate? Nay, it is not so, if we will but think. For how could it be otherwise? There is no high and noble work which a man may do in the world which does not, in its own fashion, make the same demand upon a man. Art asks from her worshippers a whole heart, and an undivided devotion. If a man have but an ounce of covetousness in him, and deflects his brush into tawdriness of treatment to win gold from the vulgar taste of the world, art will scorn such a man, and sooner or later will steal the magic from his brush. No man is lowered in his powers, said Dr. Johnson, unless he is first lowered in his tastes. When Charles Edward comes into Scotland with a mistress, he alienates the hearts of his followers. The leader of a cause must be whole-hearted in the cause. He may not bring the offering of a distracted attention to it. The divided heart is the secret of many a failure.

No! it is not a harsh thing which our Lord says. He only affirms a principle which, like most principles, is stern because it is just simple fact. If heaven were a place which could be reached by a mere change from one locality to another, then such conditions might seem harsh. If it were a matter of geography, there would seem but little reason for laying down moral conditions. But seeing that heaven is really found and only found by the heavenly character, the declaration that earthly dispositions exclude men from it is just, natural, and obvious.

But this is just what the false prophet cannot see, or will not. The false prophet is the teacher who loses the ethical sense of things. To him the heaven is geographical, and the conditions of admission and exclusion are verbal. To him a man is not self-excluded by worldliness of disposition: he is admitted or shut out by the correctness or incorrectness of his shibboleth. The Churches have made new gates in the walls of Jerusalem, but it is doubtful whether any of them lead into the city. "The gates of Zion," said Origen, "may be understood as the opposite to the gates of death: therefore as one gate of death is luxury, so the gate of Zion is chastity; a gate of death again is injustice, but the gate of Zion, justice; which the prophet shewing saith: This is the gate of the Lord, the just shall go in thereat: again, the gate of death is fear, the gate of Zion, fortitude; folly is the gate of death, but wisdom is the gate of Zion" (Comm. in St. Matt). The true gate into the city is of one pearl, and that pearl is of great price, for it is the pearl of the whole heart, which is also Christ. For so the apostle speaks: "I am crucified with Christ, nevertheless I live; yet not I, but Christ liveth in me." And this thing is only fulfilled when we cease from self. For self-sacrifice is evermore the gateway into the kingdom of love, which is the kingdom of heaven; since, how can a man love who cannot sacrifice self? This, then, is the strait gate; and this also is Christ. And what He has made thus narrow, we cannot make wide. And yet the gateway is large enough for all. It is wide enough for all kinds of intellects, talents, and views. It asks only the heart, the love.

It was thus that Christ taught His disciples. The rich young man tried to enter in at the gate, but he could not, for he brought his sacks of gold with him, and he sought to bring them in; and when he found that he must either abandon them or the gate of heaven, he took away his wealth with him. He went away sorrowful, for he had great possessions. And the disciples were amazed and said, " Who then can be saved?" (St. Matt. xix. 16-30, and xx. 1-16). And then Christ, who would not have any one think that the way into heaven was barred against any, said that heaven was open to all; for He drew the picture of the vine harvest, where the fruit was so abundant that there was employment for everybody at every hour of the day. By which He meant us to understand that we live in a world in which there is plenty of good to be done, and that whosoever knows and perceives this, and obeys the voice that bids them go and work, will enter, not into the kingdom of earth, but into the kingdom of heaven. So easy and so near to simple hearts is the heaven which others thought far off and hard to reach and narrow-gated to enter into.

And this is the thing which the false prophets confuse; for they ask men to recite their belief, where Christ asks men to give their heart. And this is putting the thing the wrong way; for a man may find his creed through his heart, but never his heart through his creed; seeing that a man may recite the true creed and yet not know Christ or heaven; but we cannot know Christ or heaven without soon coming to the best of creeds. In Bunyan's great allegory, Christian came to the wicket-gate before he came to the cross. He was ready to enter the narrow gate, to resign self, and to give up all for heaven and Christ's sake before he understood all about forgiveness, and the beauty, and joy, and boundless love, and deep meaning of the cross of Christ.

False prophets there are and ever have been. But they are specious and plausible. They wear sheep's clothing; they look as though they belonged to the fold; they can repeat much of the language of Christ's religion; they can say Lord, Lord; they know their creed well; they have a fine eye for orthodoxy, and they can sniff out a heresy before others. They stand well with the world, for they can pardon much that is unchristlike, if the right phrases be used; they can allow envy and slander, if only the party language be employed; they do not object to worldliness of behaviour and character, if only the external conformities be observed. They wear the sheep's clothing; but how terribly do they ravage the flock! For they teach unchristian hatred, and heated bigotry, and rancorous speech, and uncharitable judgments. These are some of the false prophets. And there are other false prophets who use specious words of a large charity towards loose principles, and teach that Christ asks no self-denial. These break down the gate of self-sacrifice, and build instead another gate, of great bigness and width, and call it Large-mindedness, but its true name is Self-indulgence, and it leads not to the New Jerusalem, but to the City of Destruction.

In all the impressions caused by the clamour of these false prophets, it is better to come to our Lord's own test: By their fruits ye shall know them. And the apostle proclaimed the same test, but in another fashion, when he said, "If any man have not the spirit of Christ, he is none of His" (Rom. viii. 9). Wherever we meet with the Christ-like character and the Christ-like life, there we may be sure that the Christ Himself has been at work. The life which manifests Him must be His life. For men do not gather grapes of thorns or figs of thistles (Matt. vii. 16). The good fruit means a good tree, call it by what name you will. The evil fruit means a corrupt tree, disguise it as you will (verse 17).

At this point Christ throws out a thought full of consolation. The dark and heart-oppressing clouds of evil will vanish. However strong sin and corruption, wrong practices, and unrighteous ways may seem, they are but transitory; they have no lasting vitality; they are doomed to pass away.

> "Evil in its nature is decay,
> And any hour can blot it all away."

All the idle and profitless things also will go. This is our Lord's language: "Every tree that bringeth not forth good fruit is hewn down and cast into the fire" (verse 19).

But though these words are consolatory, as assuring us of the inherent weakness of all that is evil, they convey a clear and heart-stimulating warning, since they remind us that an ever-working God will not tolerate useless things. The profitless and fruitless tree has a fitting close to its career; "whose end is to be burned." There are some trees which are fit only for firewood. There are some lives which are so insignificant and so useless that they can supply no place in the great household of God. Ah! God save us from the life whose threescore years and ten show nothing for them—no moral good attained, no noble influence diffused, no kindly work achieved; which has left hungry souls unfed, and naked ones unclad, and has shown forth no gracious and brotherly ministry among men. For such is reserved the left hand of God, and the outdoor shed where the firewood is stored.

For all life, the simple law remains—service is the test of life's value. "By their fruits ye shall know them" (verse 20).

And yet what self-deceptions are practised by men. They mistake the phrase for the truth, the outward conformity for the inward reality. It is of little value that we "profess and call ourselves Christians," unless we are indeed "led into the way of truth;" it is of little use to know the creed unless we live it, or to recite our prayers unless we translate them into action; it is of small moment to hold the faith, unless we hold it in unity of spirit and in the bond of peace. "Not every one that saith unto me, Lord, Lord, shall enter into the kingdom of heaven; but he that doeth the will of my Father which is in heaven" (verse 21).

So simple is all this teaching that we might wonder how self-deception is possible; but our Lord shows how the deceitfulness may work. He tells us that it works in the difference which there is between effective Christian work and reality of Christian conviction (verse 23). Men may prophesy and do wonders in Christ's name, and yet not be recognised by Christ as His true disciples. The late Professor Mozley pointed out that there were some people who had a talent for piety as distinguished from piety of character. The truth is, that there is nothing to which energetic people give their minds in which they cannot succeed. A person of vigorous intellect and strong will may devote his powers to religious work with as much readiness as he might have done to scientific or political work; but his doing so would not make him a religious man. It is true that he is an energetic, forceful, and successful worker in religious affairs; but the spirit within him may be untouched by the love of God or the love of man. Religion is the sphere of his work, but not the delight of his heart. It is his occupation, but not his exceeding joy: it may be his livelihood, without being his life. It may even be a joy and delight to him, because it is the sphere in which his talents find their scope and win reputation and applause. It is the sphere in which he sees the spread of his influence and the ascendency of his power. All his interest and enthusiasm may be in it, but he may be far from being a religious and Christ-loving man. "The truth is, wherever there is action, effort, aim at certain objects and ends; wherever the flame of human energy mounts up; all this may gather either round a centre of pure and unselfish desire, or round a centre of egotism; and no superiority in the subject of the work can prevent the lapse into the inferior motive." Thus it happens that, in a pure and good sense moral force is lacking in a man who pursues even religious work in a self-pleasing or self-glorifying spirit. Such a man does not bring his own moral being under the influence of religion. A great gulf is fixed between his intellectual and his moral nature. His ethical taste may approve, and his understanding may appreciate the truths of religion, but they have not become the food of his soul. And yet even while this chasm exists between the two parts of his nature, he may be eminently successful. He may be approved in the Church and applauded in the congregation. He may achieve great and useful results, but the inward life is not the life of God; Christ does not dwell in him, nor he in Christ. It is still self, and not Christ which lives in him. His work, his

Christian activity, the welcoming enthusiasm of the pious souls who recognise his ability, all contribute to his self-deception. He does not pierce beneath the surface of his life; he does not investigate the spirit which animates his actions. He believes in his own goodness; he has the evidence of his success; he takes his piety for granted. But the reality is not there after all. There is an awakening for such a man. Of this Christ gives warning in the words which follow: "Many shall say unto me, Lord, Lord, have we not prophesied in Thy name, and in Thy name done many wonderful works?" All this may be true. The gifts of life may have been used in the cause of religion, while the heart of life has not been consecrated to it. The answer of the Lord of Life must be, "I never knew you" (verse 23).

We need not go far to find examples of men highly endowed and greatly influential in religious spheres but lacking the true spirit of piety. Such men are types of gifted, but ungraced, religionism. Balaam seems to have been a man of this pattern. He has the indubitable prophetic gift, but with an unconsecrated heart. He can perceive the vision of Israel's glories in the latter days. He can realise the splendour of their destiny and the invincibility of their moral position. He recognizes the measureless superiority of their ideal life above that of surrounding nations. He can see clearly enough that there is no divination nor enchantment against Jacob. But the personal revelation of God to his soul is a separate matter. God is far above, though not out of his sight. Yet if he sees Him, it is not nigh. Thus gifts used for good ends are not the same as an inspired heart. Grace is needed to consecrate the gift. It is missed for want of thought and prayer; for no gift need be left thus unblessed. "Unto every one of us," says St. Paul, "is given grace according to the measure of the gift of Christ" (Eph. iv. 7). But men of the class we speak of are betrayed by their own gifts. They use them freely and generously in a good cause. They are apparently above all selfishness. The subtle temptation of men so gifted is love of power. They may be oblivious of their material interests; they may not be money-loving, nor even applause-loving men, but they may delight in power. They like to wield wide-spread influence; to gather men under their leadership; to be the head of a party. They achieve much; they do many wonderful works; but the lust of power is in all that they do. They lack simplicity; the eye is not single; the light within them is darkened by the overmastering desire of dominion. The work done is done in Christ's name;

it is done for the sake of His Church. But for all that they are not clean-handed workers; they walk on in darkness; they are workers of iniquity, because they have prostituted sacred things to personal ends. They have exerted a dangerous influence, drawing men to self rather than leading them to Christ. The wall is daubed with untempered mortar. There is a weakness in it which will be apparent before long.

It will be seen that our Lord takes infinite and reiterated labour to impress upon His followers the profound importance of personal reality, single-mindedness in religion. He covets for them the child-like spirit, which acts faithfully and works untiringly, without thought of reward or applause, because it loves truly and deeply. He therefore cautions against the soul-weakening and rival spirits which may animate men and which ruin personal religion, like a moth which brings rottenness into a garment.

We perceive the reason for this urgency as we draw near to the close of the Sermon on the Mount. He tells us that sooner or later the testing time must come. We live in a world which is our Father's world: it is bright with His love, as earth is bright with sunshine and with rain. But we live in a world which sooner or later brings life and character to the test. Men may be content with ill-made implements, or dwell in ill-built houses; but when the implement snaps with the first attempt to use it, or when the house comes down before the strain of weather, the bad workmanship is made known.

Our Lord enforces this, which is the climax thought of His sermon, by the parable of the two builders:

"Therefore, whosoever heareth these sayings of mine, and doeth them, I will liken him unto a wise man which built his house upon a rock:

"And the rain descended, and the floods came, and the winds blew and beat upon that house, and it fell not; for it was founded on a rock.

"And every one that heareth these sayings of mine, and doeth them not, shall be likened unto a foolish man, which built his house upon the sand:

"And the rain descended, and the floods came, and the winds blew, and beat upon that house; and it fell: and great was the fall thereof" (ch. vii. 24–27.)

The contrast is between failure and success; but the moment which determines the question of failure or success is the moment of emergency. To all seeming, while the fair weather lasted the houses built by the wise man and the foolish man were equally stable and secure. It was the storm which brought the test. We must remember the weather conditions of the Holy Land. The prolonged rainless weather is suddenly broken up by the season of rain and storm. The soil is loosened by moisture; the dry beds of streams run rapid with flood; the winds rush down upon every unprotected spot. Beneath, the earth is treacherous; around, the flood is strong; above, the winds are vehement. Every part of the house is put to the test. Everything is proved in that hour. This is the time of probation. How has the man built? Now will his wisdom be justified or his folly exposed. Now will it be known whether his work can be called success or failure. All the weeks past of apparent security were untried weeks. The flimsiest built hut could have continued standing. Now is the supreme moment which proves the man and his work.

It is in such times that we appreciate the distinction between wisdom and folly. In times of security wisdom looks like folly. The precautions of Noah are derided. But wisdom supposes the worst and provides for it lest one hour of emergency prove its work to be worthless. If there had been no storm of unusual violence the Tay Bridge might have survived; but the unexpected pressure of wind revealed the weakness of the work and proved its worthlessness for its purpose. Wisdom builds for rough times; folly for fair weather only. Folly relies upon chance, and when failure comes blames circumstances. Wisdom leaves nothing to chance, builds for the worst, criticises its own work, looks well to the foundation, and so reaches a security which is above chance and change.

One characteristic of this wisdom is patience. It is not eager to build rapidly; it is only anxious to build well. It does not shirk difficulty. In difficulty it learns patience, which is one part of the builder's skill. It knows that "raw haste is half sister to delay." Patience so practised works probation (Romans v. 4). The work of patience stands in the hour of trial. So probation leads to hope.

Thus the spirit of wisdom is seen in the desire to make its work *real*. It is not content with surface work. It will go down to the roots and foundations of things. It will not be content with knowing how to do a thing. It will do it. The foolish man is content to hear, but he has no desire to do what he hears. He acquiesces, he even approves; he can discuss, but he cannot achieve. He is good on paper, as we say: he is an office general, but an ill commander on the field. He has no idea beyond theory. The wise man has tested theory in practice; he has translated precept into action. And thence in all matters comes stability. It is thus that strong characters are built. The weaker and less tenacious are content with hearing; the more earnest desire to do. Thus, through activity their powers gain strength—their powers of work and their powers of perception: their powers of work, since powers used gain force; their powers of perception, since some knowledge is only fully gained in practice.

> "What to thought a veil may prove
> That an action may remove;
> Thus by doing you shall know
> What it is you have to do."

And this principle is one which our Lord affirmed. "If any man willeth to do His will, he shall know of the teaching, whether it be of God" (John vii. 17). It is the willingness to do which enables men to perceive the divine origin of truth. St. John expresses the same when he says that obedience is a sort of verification of God's presence. "Hereby know we that we know Him, if we keep His commandments" (1 John ii. 3).

There is a stability of understanding which arises from stability of character, for which reason a vigorous mind and a vigorous character often go hand in hand. Remembering these things we shall realise the wisdom in these words of Christ:

THE TESTS OF LIFE

"Every one that heareth these words of mine, and doeth them, shall be likened unto a wise man, which built his house upon a rock."

The end which is desired by our Lord is that true, firm, loyal, loving character which can stand in the evil day. Life tests all things, and tests character perhaps most of all. Conduct may be three parts of life, but character is five parts of conduct, and holds sway over other realms of life. It is character which determines the quality of our joys; and it is in this sense true that heaven is character. The reason that we must do as well as hear the sayings of Christ is not in any merit in the doing, but rather in the simple fact that to hear without doing is to reveal deep defect of character. The lack of action betrays the weakness and insincerity of the character, as action itself consolidates the character and deepens its earnestness. The reason we deplore those sad moral catastrophes which sometimes occur in the life of a man seemingly good and upright is because they reveal the rottenness of character which lay behind specious and pleasing behaviour. Life has tested him, and he has gone to pieces under the test.

When, then, we ask, What does our Lord signify by the falling of the one house and the firm standing of the other? we feel that the answer must be the manifestation of character which takes place through the action of testing circumstances. It is not, like St. Paul's comparison of the fire and the building, a test applied to a man's work: the test is applied to the man himself. The man is likened to the building; and the building has been well built or ill built, according to the wisdom or folly of the man in action. The fall of the building is the fall of the man, when his character is disclosed to be not what it seemed. Moreover, as all joy is dependent on character, that being no joy to one character which occasions exquisite joy to another, it follows that it is only in the character which can endure and surmount circumstances that the highest and truest joys are to be found. Here that word of the apostle (Rom. viii. 28), "All things work together for good to them that love God," may fitly be quoted. Circumstances do not always improve character; but, if the character be a fit one, circumstances strengthen it. Cornelius Agrippa, called the Magician, perceived this. In treating of the origin of evil, he said that evil material receiving holy influences turns them to its hurt. The stars work diversely on diverse souls. The rays of Saturn, which might dispose one man to obstinacy and blasphemy, might make a sound head steadier. Character counts in the result. So says St. Paul, and he only echoes Christ's teaching.

In the end every character will be disclosed: the secret rottenness which the world never dreamed of; the worldliness which was concealed under the show of philanthropy; the ambition which hid behind the veil of piety; the secret things will be made manifest. Some storms may have been weathered; but the testing storms will come sooner or later, and then the life which has not been practically good, and the character which has been content with keeping up appearances will be exposed. He alone will stand in that day who has turned his moral and religious belief into practice, who has sought to be that which he has desired or seemed to be.

Happiness is in character; character is affirmed in conduct. The circle of our Lord's teaching carries us back to the starting place. He opened (Matt. v. 3-11) by affirming that happiness was to be found rather in the inward disposition than in possession or acquisition. He closes by saying that men may build up the character which can endure and therefore can enjoy life. And in this He brings His teaching into harmony with the circle of His beatitudes. In the last beatitude He affirmed the necessity of a disposition which could endure: "Blessed are they that are persecuted for righteousness' sake;" consistently, at the close of His sermon

He speaks of the victory of the character which can endure. Happiness consists in being like our Father in heaven; and the likeness is not complete unless there be an enduring quality in it, for that which fades and abides not does not belong to the eternal kingdom. But that which is of God abides for ever; and therefore righteousness and love, when wrought into character, give it a lasting power against the assaults of temptation and trial. The crown of life belongs to such; for so wrote St. James: "Blessed is the man that endureth temptation, for when he hath been approved, he shall receive the crown of life which the Lord hath promised to them that love Him" (James i. 12).

www.ingramcontent.com/pod-product-compliance
Lightning Source LLC
Chambersburg PA
CBHW032053220426
43664CB00008B/984